CAKE DECORATING AND SUGARCRAFT

Cake Decorating and Sugarcraft

EVELYN WALLACE

NEWNES : LONDON

First published 1967

*Made and printed in Great Britain for George Newnes Ltd,
Tower House, Southampton Street, London, W.C.2 by C. Tinling & Co. Ltd,
Liverpool, London and Prescot.*

Contents

Foreword

Since I have known Evelyn Wallace I have tried to persuade her to put into a book her experience of teaching cake decoration. It is with very great pleasure, therefore, that I write the Foreword to this book which covers most of the craft work involved in decorating with sugar.

Mrs. Wallace has first-class qualifications in Domestic Science and has taught with a number of Education authorities in Lancashire, Cheshire, Northamptonshire and in County Dublin. She was for a period of ten years Joint Editress of the Irish magazine *Model Housekeeping*, and now teaches with the London County Council and Kent Education Authority.

I have, during the past eight years, had frequent opportunity to observe Mrs. Wallace at work, teaching in colleges and institutes in South East England, and I am sure there is no better person qualified to teach cake decoration. I am very grateful to her for all the work she has done, not only in teaching her craft to hundreds of housewives, but also in training some of her students to become teachers of cake decoration.

This book should prove invaluable to students in schools and colleges of Domestic Science, as well as to the housewife and home cake decorator. It is exceptionally comprehensive and covers every aspect of decorating everyday and special occasion cakes.

J. H. Thomas, B.A.

Principal of Evening Institutes
Kent County Council, Division 2
Divisional Education Office
Chislehurst, Kent

Acknowledgements

It is my hope that students, and everyone interested in decorating cakes, especially those wishing to teach themselves this fascinating art, will read this book from the beginning, because it has been written as a progressive work. The early steps of simple everyday cake icing give practice for the more difficult decorative processes used in the later designs.

Most of the cakes photographed have been made by students in my classes and are therefore not necessarily all perfect examples, but all serve to show the success which can be achieved, and to show how effective some of the simplest work can look. The ambitious students have put in hours of practice to achieve the more elaborately decorated cakes illustrated towards the back of the book, and I should like to say thank you here to all my students at Bromley Technical College, Eltham Institute, and Orpington Evening Institute for the special interest they have all shown in their work—it has given me, personally, a real satisfaction.

Most of the photographs in this book are by Mr Derek Davis, to whom I am indebted for his patience and help. I also wish to thank Messrs Tate & Lyle for the photographs shown in plates *6, 7* and *10, 12* to *17*, and *18* to *23*; Messrs Cadbury Bros., for the Easter egg photograph shown in plate **14**, Mr C. G. Brown for the photographs shown in plates **54, 55**, *191, 193* and *195*, and Mr John E. Williams for the photographs shown in plates *34, 37, 50, 59, 97, 99* and *166*. Last but not least I owe a special debt to my students, and particularly to Mrs Margaret Neale who typed out the pages of hand written notes.

Orpington, 1967   EVELYN WALLACE

Introduction

This is a book which sets out to teach a craft and encourage an art, for perfection in cake icing involves a degree of both. Craftsmanship plays a great part in cake decoration—this book aims to bring out the latent creative ability that is in every person, and to use it to perfect a craft. By following correctly a series of progressive lessons in cake decoration, it is amazing what the amateur can achieve.

Producing a cake at a party, which has its own attractive theme design, is in itself, its own reward—it creates an unexpected amount of pleasure and delight. Even the simplest decoration can be rewarding when friends admire a birthday or tea-time cake made especially for their visit. This simple work encourages efforts at more ambitious pieces, and gradually fascination takes over.

It would be futile to say that elaborate pieces of craftsmanship can be produced without practice. It is like the production of a work for a concert—constant practice is required. But becoming proficient in cake icing is a joy and very rewarding.

Someone once said: "Knowledge without practice makes but half an artist—skill is a treasure, but practice is the key to it." There is no drudgery in the practice, because an iced cake not quite up to standard tastes just as good as another cake, and is soon eaten. A different design is produced next time and almost any idea can be portrayed in cake decoration. The themes are almost unlimited.

Colour plays a great part in sugar-craft, and the ambitious student will try to produce a colour delicacy to match the surroundings in which the cake is to be served. Fine lines of over-piping in colour can alter or emphasise the whole appearance of a cake and may sometimes even surprise the decorator. A favourite bar of music can be put on the side or top of a special anniversary cake. A school or college badge makes an interesting centre piece for a boy's birthday cake. Hand piped flowers can be very realistic and never fail to gain admiration on a girl's birthday cake. A nursery rhyme portrayed in coloured icing delights both mothers and children at a nursery tea party. Wedding cakes with the bride and bridgegroom's skills or interests illustrated in sugar make a never-to-be-forgotten cake, with a personal interest. Each idea becomes more fascinating as the work proceeds and more skill is achieved.

It is the aim of this book to teach the making of the various icings, together with their uses. Although a number of designs are suggested, the idea is to give the students a sufficient working knowledge so that individual ideas can then be carried out easily and successfully. Sugarcraft is an outlet for creative expression—a means of enjoyment. Just as pleasure can be obtained from reading, painting or embroidery, so it can also be found in this new form of art and craft.

The suggestions in this book—novelty cakes, boxes of candies, sugar dainties—each one makes an unusual gift for "the friend who has everything". A gift which is so individual and personal that it is more acceptable than silk or silver. And far more rewarding.

Part One

PUBLISHER'S NOTE

The black-and-white plates in this book are numbered and referred to by italic figures, thus pl. *1*; the colour plates by bold figures, thus pl. **1**.

CHAPTER ONE

Icings and How to Use Them

Before beginning to ice a cake, it is
necessary to decide what effect it is
desired to create. Consider the occasion,
the icing, and the type of cake to be
decorated. Step by step in this book, each
type of icing is described—the way it is
made and the way in which it should be
used.

There are numerous types of icings and
frostings, all suitable for different cakes
and different occasions. These first three
chapters will cover a few of them: *glacé
icing*, sometimes called water icing; *fudge
icing*, a popular soft icing; *caramel icing*, a
delicious flavoured, soft icing; *American
frosting*; *boiled fondant*, used mainly by
confectioners; *Vienna icing*, sometimes
called butter cream; *almond icing*, also
known as almond paste or marzipan; *cold
fondant*; and *royal icing*, a hard-setting
icing, always used on wedding cakes.

GLACÉ ICING

Glacé icing is an easy to make, everyday
icing. It can be used on yeast buns, as a
small centre on cup cakes, decorated with
a cherry, or on flat-topped Victoria and
sponge sandwiches, Madeira and light
fruit cakes. It is not suitable for rich fruit
cakes.

Ingredients:

Icing sugar.
A little hot water.

Method: To make glacé icing for the top
of a cake, use about one ounce of icing
sugar to each inch of cake: an eight-inch
cake takes about eight ounces of icing
sugar. For good results never use too little
sugar. Put the sugar, unsifted, into a basin

and add almost boiling water from the
kettle. Stir with a wooden spoon until
enough water has been added to make a
creamy consistency to coat the back of the
spoon with icing. Stir well until all the
sugar is absorbed, but avoid beating,
which causes air bubbles. If coloured
icing is required, use a skewer dipped into
a bottle of edible colour—never add colour
to icing by pouring straight from the
bottle. Stir the icing well so that it is
evenly mixed, but avoid taking too long or
it will cool and not set well on the cake.

Place the cake to be iced ready on a
doyley on a plate to prevent disturbing the
icing later.

Pour all the icing onto the cake, coaxing
it across the top with a dry knife—a wet
knife leaves pools of water. Avoid pulling
up the surface of the cake. Bring the icing
just to the edge by turning the cake all the
time. If the icing is too thin and runs down
the sides, never try to scoop it up—this
prevents setting. Leave the icing to dry
and then cut off any surplus. With
experience icing can be mixed to just the
right consistency to be coaxed to the edge
of the cake and remain neat.

To glacé ice the sides of a cake

If the side of the cake is to be iced this
should be done before the top, and coated
with nuts or chocolate vermicelli—plain
icing does not usually look very attractive
on the side of the cake.

The easiest way to obtain a professional
finish is to have ready some flaked or
chopped and toasted almond nuts, chopped
walnuts or toasted or coloured coconut.
To toast the nut, place on a metal plate
under a hot grill or in a medium hot oven,
and allow to brown nicely, stirring frequently with a spoon to prevent burning

and to obtain an even colour. Coconut may be coloured by putting two or three drops of edible colouring into a plateful of coconut and rubbing in the colour by hand until it is evenly mixed. Put the nuts on a sheet of greaseproof paper ready to use.

Meanwhile, put two or three tablespoonfuls of icing sugar into a small basin and add a very little hot water to make the glacé icing. Spread the icing on the sides of the cake with a knife and roll in the nuts until evenly coated, pressing the nuts gently to the sides of the cake. As a cheaper decoration, use toasted oatmeal or crushed breakfast cereal, toasted cake or biscuit crumbs. Grated or curled chocolate or chocolate vermicelli can be used in place of the nuts. Jam or butter cream may be used in place of the icing.

Remember that it is essential for the best results, to complete the sides of a cake before attempting to begin work on the top. If a filling of jam or cream is to be used, always cut the cake after the sides have been coated and before the top is iced. If the cake is moved after glacé icing is put on the top surface, it will probably crack or wrinkle. Keeping a cake for a few days after icing can also cause wrinkling as the natural drying out process moves the icing.

To bake a good cake for icing, use a sufficiently thin mixture, and an oven which is not too hot, so that the finished cake has an even, flat surface. If it has risen in the centre, turn it over and ice the bottom. The rounded cake top may well fit into a deep plate, but if not, a slice can always be cut off the top to make a good level surface—but to ice a cut surface successfully, it must first be brushed with apricot glaze to set the crumbs.

To make apricot glaze

With a teaspoon rub some apricot jam through a tea-strainer into a small basin. Stand the basin in a pan of hot water, and when thoroughly hot, brush across the top of the cake and allow to set before icing. If the jam is very thick, stand the jar in hot water before sieving, or add a few drops of water to make the glaze

spread easily. If the cake is to be kept a long time, boil the glaze after the water is added, otherwise it may go mouldy.

Cherry cake using glacé icing (see pl. 1)

Glacé ice the top of the cake over the set apricot glaze, and when the icing is set, decorate with cherries, angelica, nuts, or any other designs ingenuity suggests. Stems of angelica can be used with half cherries arranged as a branch in the cake centre, or as smaller bunches round the edge. The following diagrams show ideas for decoration using cherries and angelica.

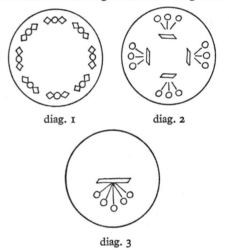

diag. 1   diag. 2

diag. 3

Flavoured, as well as coloured icing, can be made simply by adding a few drops of essence of vanilla, essence of almond, rose water, orange flower water or peppermint essence, or orange or lemon juice, diluted to taste with very hot water. Icing sugar mixed with strong black coffee or strong cocoa produce good coffee and chocolate icing—add a small piece of butter to chocolate icing to give a shiny surface. Melted chocolate may also be used in place of icing.

Orange or lemon cakes using glacé icing

Using a potato peeler, peel the rind off a fresh orange. Squeeze the juice from the orange, strain, and heat gently in a saucepan. Mix icing sugar with the hot juice and carefully coat the top of the cake with the mixture. With scissors cut tiny rounds of peel to look like little oranges and use these with pieces of angelica to decorate the cake. Strained lemon juice heated with hot water can also be used, decorating the cake with angelica and lemon shapes cut from the peel. Alternatively tiny cocktail cutters can be used to make various shapes.

Domino cake using glacé icing (see pl. *2)*

Bake a cake in a loaf tin using a Madeira mixture. If necessary, cut the top level and brush with apricot glaze. Spread the sides of the cake with a little glacé icing and coat with toasted nuts. Place the cake on a doyley on a plate and pour white glacé icing on the top surface. Coax the icing just to the edge and allow to set.

Cut two strips of paper two inches wide and the length of the width of the cake. Place the papers across the cake about one-eighth of an inch apart. Shave some chocolate finely with a knife and sprinkle between the inside edges of the paper. Press gently with the fingers—this makes the line on the top of the domino. Remove the paper and arrange chocolate buttons for the spots on the domino.

For small domino cakes, bake the mixture in a large flat tin. Ice all over the top with glacé icing and when set cut into strips about three inches wide. Make a line of chocolate as in the larger cake—or pipe a line of chocolate icing—down the centre of the length of each strip. Remove the paper and cut each strip across into fingers about one inch wide, wiping the knife before each new cake is cut. Use small pieces of chocolate or chocolate button *Polka Dots* for decorating domino numbers, or pipe the dots with chocolate icing. Place the individual cakes in paper cases to give an attractive finish.

FUDGE ICING

This is a popular soft-textured icing generally used for less formal designs. It can be poured over a cake during the beating process, just before thickening, or with extra beating it can be made to take patterns using a knife or serrated scraper, as in diags. 4–7. It is an ideal icing for fillings, or for covering sponge cakes, Genoese sponges, Madeira and plain type cakes, or very light fruit cakes. Again, this is not suitable for rich fruit cakes.

Ingredients:

> ½ lb. icing sugar.
> 1½ ozs. margarine or butter.
> 4 dessertspoons milk or cream.
> 3 drops vanilla essence, or 2 teaspoons instant coffee or 2 teaspoons cocoa.
> Pinch of salt.

Method: Sift the icing sugar into a bowl. Melt the butter or margarine slowly, but do not boil or allow to separate. Add the milk or cream and salt, and heat gently to 160°F. or just below simmering point. Keep at this temperature for two minutes and add the vanilla. Pour all at once over the sugar and beat until stiff. For coating the cake top and sides, pour over quickly just as the icing is beginning to stiffen—for making a pattern, beat the mixture a little longer. For coffee or chocolate fudge icing, pour the hot liquid very quickly over the instant coffee or cocoa and stir. Pour into the sugar all at once while still hot, and beat as before. As well as making a good top icing, this makes an excellent filling for a cake.

The quantities given above will coat a seven-inch cake top and sides. For a filling as well, double the quantity. Mark the top with a knife, fork, or serrated scraper in a pattern, as for butter cream. Decorate with walnuts or cherries and angelica leaves.

CARAMEL ICING

This is a richly-flavoured icing used effectively on the top and sides of a cake or as a filling. It is most suitable for plain type cakes like sponges, Madeiras, or light sultana, cherry or walnut cakes.

Ingredients to cover a seven-inch cake:

    5 tablespoons of creamy milk.
    3 ozs. butter.
    2 tablespoons castor sugar.
    12 ozs. sifted icing sugar.

Method: Sift the icing sugar into a bowl. Heat the castor sugar gently in a small, heavy saucepan, until a caramel is formed. Melt the butter in a second saucepan, but avoid boiling or separating. Add the milk to the butter and bring to 160°F., or just below simmering point. Pour into the caramel pan. Stir until all the caramel is dissolved. Pour over the icing sugar and beat until the icing is smooth and creamy and thick enough to spread. Have the cake cut through the centre, ready to put in a layer of the icing quickly. Sandwich together and coat the top and sides.

Mark the top of the cake with a fork, knife, or serrated scraper, using any of the patterns given for butter cream. Decorate with nuts, etc.

AMERICAN FROSTING

This icing is crisp outside and soft inside. It can be used as a filling, as a soft smooth coating, or, with longer beating, as a rocky coating, although it is not hard like royal icing. A sugar thermometer is necessary for first-class results. This frosting is most suitable for the plainer types of cake.

Ingredients:

    1 lb. loaf sugar.
    ¼ pt. cold water.
    2 egg whites.
    Decorations—nuts, cherries or angelica.

Method: Place the sugar in the water and leave to stand a while in a pan. As this icing sets at once when it is made, have ready all the decorations and place the cake on an upturned plate or wire rack ready for icing. Place the pan over a gentle heat and make sure the sugar is completely dissolved before allowing it to boil. Bring the temperature up to 240°F. Meanwhile,

using a hand whisk or an electric beater, beat the egg whites until very stiff. When the syrup has reached 240°F., allow the bubbles to subside and pour the syrup over the egg whites, beating all the time. With a hand whisk it takes two people to make this frosting. Beat until the icing is very thick and fluffy and will pull up into peaks, and then spread quickly on the cake. If wanted for filling also, have the cake separated into two or three layers and cover all the layers. Decorate the top quickly and place the layers together.

For a smoother surface, remove the beater from the icing a few minutes earlier, when the mixture will coat the back of a spoon. Place the cake on a wire rack, pour the frosting over it and leave to set—this icing will not be suitable for filling.

American frosting is not an easy icing to make. It requires practice to learn to know its appearance, and produce good results. If needed, colouring may also be added.

To prevent graining—the sugar becoming hard or crystalizing on the sides of the pan—a pastry brush dipped in cold water should be used to brush the sides of the pan as the sugar is boiling.

BOILED FONDANT ICING

Fondant icing has a delicious, mellow flavour, and keeps far better than glacé icing. It is used an enormous amount by confectioners, but it can be used by the home cook for coating small or large cakes, and sometimes as a base for royal icing. But for good results, a sugar thermometer *must* be used.

Ingredients:

    1 lb. loaf sugar.
    1¼ gills water (1 gill = ¼ pint).
    1 tablespoon glucose or pinch of cream of tartar.

Method: Place the sugar and water in a saucepan and leave to stand while the sugar softens—overnight if possible. Place in a covered pan over a gentle heat to dissolve

1. *Right*—Sponge cake with glacé icing, decorated with cherries and angelica.

2. *Below*—Domino cake covered with glacé icing.

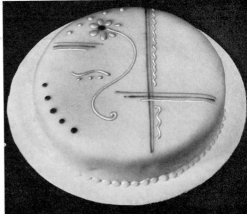

3. *Above*—A cake covered and decorated entirely with boiled fondant icing.

4. *Left*—Sponge cake being decorated with butter icing using a serrated scraper and chocolate mushrooms.

5. *Left*—A chocolate log using a swiss roll and butter cream. Also marzipan being cut into holly leaves for decoration on the log.

6. *Centre left*—Use a palette-knife to press the almond paste firmly to the cake—as demonstrated by a chef.

7. *Centre Right*—Trim the strip of almond paste neatly and roll the round cake along it. Make a neat join and then place on the cake drum.

8. *Left*—Alternative design for simnel cake or 'Mother's Day' cake.

9. *Left*—Cake iced and decorated with cold fondant in white and red indented with a serrated scraper and finished with gay silver braid.

10. *Right*—Correct icing equipment should always be on hand: cake boards, turntable, mixing bowl and spoon, scales, icing bags and tubes, palette-knife, wooden spatula, egg separator and measuring rings.

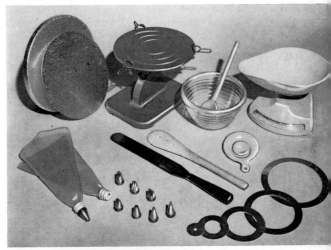

11. *Left*—Alternative design for simnel cake or 'Mother's Day' cake.

12.   Royal icing, well beaten and at the correct consistency for piping, as demonstrated by a chef.

13.   Royal icing at the correct consistency for coating an almond pasted cake.

14.   Royal icing spread evenly over the cake surface with a palette-knife.

15.   Air is released from the icing by a backwards and forwards movement.

16.   Knife at right angles to board smoothing cake sides.

17.   Alternative method of smoothing icing across cake top with knife or ruler as demonstrated by a chef.

the sugar without stirring. Do not allow the sugar to boil. After two minutes remove the lid and add glucose or a pinch of cream of tartar dissolved in one teaspoon of water. Put the sugar thermometer in the saucepan and when all the sugar is quite dissolved, bring to the boil slowly, brushing the side of the pan with cold water to prevent crystals forming. Boil steadily to 240°F., remove from the heat at once and allow the bubbles to subside. Have ready a cold, wet, marble slab, or if not possible, use a large, cold, wet, bowl. Pour the sugar mixture steadily in a thin stream onto the slab or into the bowl. Using a wooden or stainless steel spatula, work the fondant from the outside into the middle until white and firm. If the icing is in a bowl, leave it to cool a little before beating well. When the mixture begins to set, take up pieces and knead well until smooth. Put the pieces in a screw-top jar, screw down when cold and store until required.

To use the fondant

Have the cakes ready on a wire tray—small cakes should be brushed with hot apricot glaze or covered with a thin layer of almond icing. Large cakes need not be covered unless there are loose crumbs. Fondant icing is only suitable for the lighter cakes like Madeira or sponges, unless a covering of almond paste has been used first.

Make a stock syrup with a pound of sugar to three-quarters of a pint of water. Heat together till all sugar is dissolved, and then bring to the boil. Brush the sides of the pan with cold water to prevent the sugar crystallizing.

Put some of the fondant icing into a double saucepan and add a little of the stock syrup. When the mixture coats the back of the spoon and is about 80°F. to 85°F. it is ready for use.

Put the cakes on a wire tray and pour the fondant icing steadily over them. Smooth as quickly as possible. Fondant icing can also be used for simple piping on small or large cakes (pl. *3*). The stock syrup can be used up for making lemonade

or orangeade, put into fruit salads, or stored for future use. The fondant in the jar keeps well and becomes more mellow with storing. Colourings and flavourings can always be added.

Ready-made fondant icing can be bought, but take care not to over-heat when re-warming and thinning.

BUTTER CREAM OR VIENNA ICING

This is easy to make and can be used as a decoration or as a filling. It can be flavoured and coloured and used on plain Madeira cakes, sponge sandwiches or Genoese cakes—not rich fruit cakes.

Ingredients to cover an eight-inch cake:

    8 ozs. butter or margarine.
    8 ozs. sifted icing sugar.
    Colouring and flavouring to taste.
    1 tablespoon evaporated milk (optional).

Method: Cream together equal quantities of salted, or fresh unsalted margarine or butter and sifted icing sugar—if preferred, the salt can be removed from salted margarine or butter by folding it in butter muslin, standing in cold water for a time, and then kneading it, still in the muslin, under cold running water or in a bowl of fresh water, to remove any remaining salt. For a sweeter icing, use up to twice as much sugar as margarine, but the equal quantity recipe is better for piping. Any flavourings can be used—vanilla, almond essence, lemon or orange juice or squash, rosewater, orange flower water, violet or peppermint flavourings, strong black coffee, instant coffee or cocoa. It is best too, that the colouring should match the flavouring: orange colour and orange flavouring, a pink colour and rose flavouring or green colouring and peppermint flavouring.

This butter cream is ideal for a quick, simple cake. A knife, fork or serrated scraper can be used to give an attractive finish (pl. *4*).

Diagrams showing designs which can be obtained by using a knife

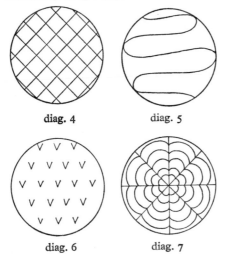

diag. 4   diag. 5

diag. 6   diag. 7

When carrying out these designs, first put a filling of butter cream and jam in the cake, and then spread the top of the cake with butter cream as evenly as possible with a palette knife. Avoid pulling up cake crumbs into the icing. It is a good plan to brush with apricot glaze first and allow to set. For diagrams:

4. Mark the cake top with lines as if cutting the cake in a diamond pattern. Keep wiping the knife free from butter cream.

5. Using the end of a small palette or dinner knife, bring the knife backwards and forwards to give this effect.

6. Use the flat side of the palette knife and pull up the butter cream in even points.

7. Make circular indentations all round the cake, then draw the point of the knife from the centre to the outside or from the outside to the centre, in eight positions. This fundamental method can be varied to make a variety of patterns.

To add a finishing touch to these designs, dredge the top lightly with fine icing sugar or sprinkle with chocolate vermicelli or coloured granulated sugar—sprinkle a few drops of edible colour on granulated sugar on a saucer and rub together with the fingers.

After decoration, put the cake in a cool place for the icing to harden. Butter cream has a high fat content and is liable to melt or become very soft if exposed to too great a heat.

To make a chocolate log, using butter cream (pl. 5)

Ingredients:

> 2 to 3 ozs. margarine.
> 2 to 3 ozs. sifted icing sugar.
> 1 tablespoon cocoa (more if a darker colour is required).
> A little vanilla essence.
> 1 chocolate roll.
> 2 teaspoons evaporated milk (optional).

Method: Make or buy a chocolate roll. Cream the margarine with the sifted icing sugar until very light. Add sifted cocoa to taste, until a nice dark colour, and flavour with vanilla essence. Beat in the evaporated milk. Spread the cream thickly on the top and sides of the roll and mark with a fork to represent the bark of a tree. Decorate with sprigs of marzipan holly or ivy leaves made from marzipan—*see* Chapter Two—and a robin or woodpecker.

To make a log with a branch, cut a corner off the roll for one branch, or a corner from each end for two branches or knots.

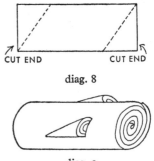

CUT END   CUT END

diag. 8

diag. 9

Place the cut side to the roll, joining and covering with a little butter cream so that the branch is "growing" at the correct angle from the roll.

Mark the icing with a fork so that the bark on the branch is in keeping with the bark on the log. Place the log on an oblong silver board. There are several ingenious ways of decorating these cakes.

To make an alpine roll

Using a plain sponge roll and white butter cream, follow the method given for the chocolate log. Smooth the cream with a knife and pull up in points to represent snow. Decorate with snow babies modelled from white marzipan made from ground almonds, white of egg and sugar. Paint pink faces using edible colour, and using a dark red colouring give the little figures eyes and shoes and rosebud mouths. Blue, red and green edible colour will give the dark colour if mixed in very small quantity. A fine, small, artist's brush should be used for painting the face.

To make chocolate mushrooms (pl. 4)

Make some chocolate buns using the chocolate cake recipe at the back of the book, but putting only a teaspoonful in each tin. The buns should be flat on one side and rounded on the other. Make up some almond paste—about two or three ounces will cover twelve mushrooms. Roll out the almond paste thinly and cut into rounds with a biscuit cutter. Lightly coat the rounds of almond paste with apricot jam and press over the rounded side of the bun. This represents the top of the mushroom. Have ready some butter cream and add a little cocoa to make the colour of the mushroom gills. Spread the butter cream thickly onto the flat side of the bun and line with a fork from the centre outwards. Roll the remaining almond paste into a thin, round strip, and cut off the number of mushroom "stalks" needed. Press into the centre of each upturned mushroom.

CHAPTER TWO

The Technique of Almond Paste or Marzipan

This chapter explains the technique of making and using almond icing or almond paste, equally well known as marzipan. It is most often used as a foundation for royal icing on wedding or birthday cakes, to prevent the rich cake from staining the white surface. But besides this practical function, almond paste can be used as a decoration in its own right, to make interesting and unusual designs in a variety of colours, and to mould flowers and figures.

Ingredients:

> 1 lb. ground almonds.
> 1 lb. castor sugar.
> 1 lb. icing sugar.
> 2 large or 3 small eggs, or 4 yolks of eggs if the whites are to be saved for royal icing.

These quantities will cover a nine-inch cake. If the cake is to be kept for some time, add a tablespoon of spirits—rum, brandy, or whisky, or a little lemon juice or orange flower water to the almond paste.

Method: Sift the two sugars into a bowl and add the ground almonds. Mix well. Make a well in the centre of the mixture, add the spirits if used, and then add the well-beaten eggs gradually, stirring with a wooden spoon. Make into a stiff paste, adding only the necessary amount of liquid. If the paste is too soft it will be difficult to handle. Knead lightly until smooth, but avoid over-kneading as this can cause the almond paste to become greasy.

To put almond paste on a cake

Dredge some cornflour onto the baking board and turn out all the paste. Form into a ball and divide in half, using one half for the top of the cake. Using the hands, shape to fit the top of the cake, and roll out, using a little cornflour sprinkled on the rolling pin. If necessary, slice the top of the cake quite level, making sure that no crumbs touch the almond paste.

Spread the almond paste evenly almost to the edges with apricot jam, avoiding using the fruit skin. Make sure that it is loose from the baking board. Place the cake upside down on the almond paste, press firmly (pl. *6*), and then carefully turn the whole thing over. In this way a nice flat top is assured, as the almond paste will take on the shape of the cake.

When icing a round cake, divide the remaining piece of almond paste into two —four for a square cake. Roll into sausage shapes until each is long enough to encircle half the cake, or until each is the length of one side of a square cake. Use a piece of string to measure the round cake. Roll out the sausage shape to the right depth, measuring the depth of the cake with a knife, and spread the strips with apricot jam. Place the cake onto the strips, similar to the top. Roll a round cake along the strips, making a neat join (pl. *7*). Work on the cake with the rolling pin to make a neat finish—the better the result of the almond paste, the easier it will be to obtain a good finish to the white icing. Use a straight-sided jar rolled against the side of the cake for a perfectly upright cake side. Work similarly for a square cake.

Put the cake onto a thick silver board or cake drum, cover with a tin and allow to dry for four or five days. Always allow the air to dry it a little, otherwise the grease may come through the royal icing and show a stain.

in the icing. Finally, arrange a paper frill round the sides of the cake.

SIMNEL CAKE

OR MOTHERS' DAY CAKE
(pls. *8* and *11*)

Always use a rich fruit cake mixture, putting half the mixture into a baking tin and keeping back the other half.

Make up half a pound of almond paste and cut into two pieces. Roll out one piece into a flat cake to fit the tin. Place this on the cake mixture already in the tin. Fill up with the rest of the cake mixture. Hollow out the top of the cake mixture but avoid disturbing the almond paste. Bake in the usual way. To tell when the cake is done, make sure the top is firm to touch—the skewer test is not satisfactory, as the almond paste is always sticky and would remain on the skewer.

From the remaining piece of almond paste, make a roll long enough to encircle the edge of the cake. Brush the cake edge with jam and fit on the roll of almond paste, pressing it firmly and neatly. Prick the top edge with a fork and brush with beaten egg. Tie greased paper round the edge of the cake, protecting the centre with a piece of foil, and place it in a hot oven or under the grill, turning frequently until the almond paste is evenly browned.

When the cake is quite cold, fill the centre of the ring of almond paste with glacé icing or thin royal icing. Arrange piped flowers in a spray in the centre, or decorate the top with a marzipan nest (*see* Chapter Four), or cherries and angelica. Large round balls or eggs of marzipan are often placed round the edge of the cake in place of the roll, but make sure the balls touch each other, otherwise the icing will run out between them, and down the sides of the cake.

If the cake is to be kept for a long time, a thin layer of almond paste put under the icing gives a better foundation. Allow the almond paste to dry a little before pouring

BATTENBERG CAKE

Prepare a Madeira cake or Victoria sandwich recipe, using two eggs. Have ready two oblong, straight-sided tins, about eight inches long by three inches wide. Put half the mixture in a greased and lined tin, and using edible colouring, colour the rest of the mixture pink. Put the pink mixture in the second tin and bake as for Victoria sandwich.

When cold, trim each cake in half, lengthwise, taking off a thin outer crust. Sandwich the four lengths together, using apricot jam, so that the pink is over the yellow and vice-versa, forming a square at each end, with four panes like a window. Press together firmly.

Roll out half a pound of almond paste to a neat square and spread with apricot jam. Place the prepared cake on the almond paste or marzipan, and fold the paste round the side of the cake. Make a neat join along one edge of the cake. Trim with a knife and define the edges of the finished cake with a fork or by pinching with the finger and thumb. Decorate with cherries and angelica.

The cake trimmings and any scraps of marzipan can always be used to make a trifle using fruit juice, with custard and cream.

MARQUETRY WITH MARZIPAN
(pl. *1*)

Experiment with the fascinating patterns that can be made using marzipan as a top decoration in itself, most suitable on a sponge or light fruit cake. Cut a circle or square of paper to fit the top of the cake, fold the paper in half, in half again, and in half again, so that when opened out, there are eight folded sections (diag. 10). Now divide these sections by drawing lines through each one, to form a geometrical pattern (diag. 11)—there is no end to the possibilities.

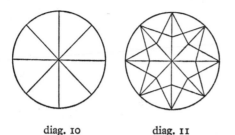

diag. 10   diag. 11

Now decide on the way in which colour will give most effect to the pattern. Trace the pattern onto a piece of tracing or greaseproof paper, and cut out each section, numbering according to the planned colour, *e.g.*, number all green sections 1, all pink, 2, etc.

Colour some of the marzipan pink, and roll out to a quarter of an inch thickness, using a little cornflour on the board. Using the sections of paper numbered 2, cut out corresponding shapes of the pink marzipan and place them on the original pattern. Continue with the green paste in the same way, until all the sections are completed.

Coat the sides of the cake with jam, and roll in toasted nuts. Fill in any cracks on the top of the cake with marzipan, making a good surface as the marzipan will take the shape of the cake. Spread with jam, lift the pattern pieces carefully from the paper, and place one by one in position on the cake. Take care not to stretch the marzipan or spoil the shape in any way. When the pattern is completed, gently rub the surface with the hand to neaten the joins. The finished cake should resemble plate 1.

To make the second cake illustrated, the box pattern must be worked out carefully on paper before beginning to work with the paste. For special occasions, scenes can be cut out illustrating special events and objects. Children's books and old needlework books usually produce an endless fund of good pattern ideas.

It is possible to do this "marquetry" with a cold fondant paste, but as it is more liable to stretch out of shape, much more care is needed when placing the pieces on the cake, and it is advisable to attempt less elaborate designs.

SUGAR PASTE OR COLD FONDANT

Children are not always fond of almond paste, and cold fondant can make a very good substitute covering for all cakes, especially at children's parties when discarded marzipan is often left on the sides of the plates!

Ingredients:

> 1 lb. icing sugar.
> 1 white of egg.
> 1 to 2 ozs. liquid glucose (bought at the chemist's, this looks like a thick white or clear treacle).
> 2 to 4 teaspoons lemon juice or vanilla essence.
> 1 teaspoon glycerine if a very soft icing is required.

These quantities will cover an eight-inch cake.

Method: Sift the icing sugar into a basin. If the glucose is stiff, stand the jar in a saucepan of hot water for a few minutes. Make a well in the centre of the sugar and add the glucose, whisked white of egg, and flavouring, if used. Mix thoroughly, dust the hands with a little cornflour, and knead the mixture well, adding more sugar as required, to make a stiff paste—the amount of sugar needed will depend on the size of the egg used. Plenty of kneading will be required before the mixture has a smooth, fine texture.

Dredge the board with cornflour, and roll out the paste. Follow the directions given previously for putting almond icing on a cake, but make sure the surface is quite flat, as any unevenness will show through the cold fondant paste. With a little cornflour on the fingers, rub the top of the fondant to give a smooth, shiny, polished finish. After drying a little while, the cake may be coated with royal icing, or decorated with piping straight onto the shiny surface.

It is possible, also, to put a layer of almond paste before a top icing of cold fondant. The result is good, and the taste of the cold fondant is improved, in fact, although this method is not suitable for icing an ornate wedding cake with pillars, many people prefer it to royal icing for Christmas and birthday cakes (pls. 2 and 3).

Experiment by indenting the smooth surface of the cold fondant with a serrated scraper, and decorating with coloured flowers made from the same material. However, if cold fondant is to be used for flowers it is essential not to add glycerine as it would be too soft for modelling (pl. 9).

CHAPTER THREE

Royal Icing

Royal icing is the special occasion icing. It is hard setting, and is always used for wedding cakes and good birthday cakes. It is the best kind of icing suitable for piping designs and sugar flowers.

Always take special care and a little extra time when making royal icing so that a perfect dazzling whiteness is produced.

Preparing to make royal icing

It is most essential to see that all the utensils used—bowls, measures, spoons, spatulas, etc., are clean and free from grease (pl. *10*). When making royal icing for the first time, choose, if possible, a new white bowl about eight to ten inches across the top, with a good glaze. This basin should be used for icing only, kept perfectly clean, and stored in a paper bag when not in use. Never use a cracked or crazed bowl, or one which has been used for creaming butter and sugar or steaming puddings, or the icing will discolour.

To be sure that the bowl used is absolutely clean, rub it well with salt, place all the utensils inside, and fill with boiling water to sterilize. Stand for a few minutes, and then rinse well. Allow to dry and cool with the bowl turned upside down. Even drying the bowl with a tea towel can spoil the icing, as a thread from the cloth may be inadvertently left behind and block the icing tube, so that the icing breaks when piping fine lines. This is annoying and causes bad workmanship when piping.

For a student intending to do a lot of cake decoration, a good quality turn-table will be very useful and worth buying, but for home use, two inverted soup plates on top of each other are useful, or even a home-made turn-table. To make an "amateur" turn-table, use a round metal or tin tray about ten or twelve inches across, and two pieces of hard wood—two circular wooden teapot stands would be suitable. Make an identical circular groove in both stands and place several ball-bearings in one of them. Place the two stands together with the ball bearings held in position between the grooves. Fasten the stands with a suitable screw, having made a slightly larger hole in the upper stand to enable it to rotate freely. A washer should be placed under the screw head before assembling. Finally, drill four holes in the tray and screw it upside down onto the upper teapot stand. Any handyman should be able to make a good job of this.

Care of sugar

Icing sugar should be bought in sealed packages and stored in a dry place, not in a kitchen cupboard where there may be steam. Lumpy sugar is unsatisfactory, as sieving and rolling to remove lumps may make the sugar greasy or soiled and discolour the icing, preventing that perfect whiteness so essential on a good cake. A packet of lumpy icing sugar can always be used up for making glacé icing for a sponge cake, but *not* for royal icing.

Immediately after using the icing sugar, close up the packet and store it carefully in a dry place. The manufacturers go to much trouble preparing, packing and sealing icing sugar—the user should take a similar amount of care. One speck of dust in the sugar can ruin the beautiful whiteness of a wedding cake and take away the "untouched by hand" look that homemade cakes and sweets should have to raise them above the level of manufactured goods.

1. *Top left*—Designs in marzipan " marquetry ".

2. *Centre right*—Christmas cake using cold fondant as a top icing and as a modelling medium, over a thin layer of almond icing.

3. *Bottom left*—Birthday cake for a 99-year-old covered with cold fondant and decorated with roses modelled from cold fondant.

5. *Centre right*—Holly and candles modelled from cold fondant—the ideal decoration for a Christmas cake.

4. *Top left*—Fruits modelled from marzipan—the ideal box of sweetmeats.

6. *Bottom left*—Animals modelled in marzipan and cold fondant.

7. *Top left*—A Santa Claus cake with decoration modelled in cold fondant.

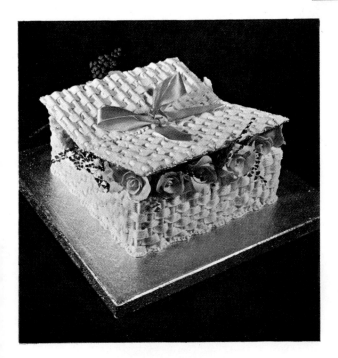

8. *Top right*—A "seagull scene" cake using white sugar birds and cake using the eight-point-star design in pink glacé icing and white royal icing.

9. *Centre left*—Basket of roses with double lid and cold fondant roses.

10. *Bottom right*—Silver wedding cake with lettering, run-out hearts, piped roses and the figures 25 on the side.

11. *Top left*—Apple blossom and trellis figures make a 21st birthday cake—make numbers by outlining on waxed paper, working trellis and outlining a second time.

12. *Top right*—Easter cake egg baked in two basins pieced together with jam and covered with cold fondant. Cockerel and primroses are piped on to waxed paper first, other decorations piped straight on to the egg.

13. *Centre right*—Valentine biscuits decorated with small tulips, primroses, narcissi and trellis and lace work icing with a run-out edge.

14. *Bottom left*—Easter eggs decorated with marzipan anemones and chocolate piping.

15. *Top left*—Tray of savoury biscuits piped with creamed cheese and savoury butters.

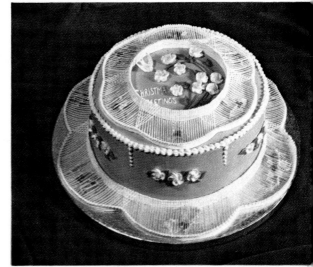

16. *Centre right*—Christmas cake with built up centre of fine lines over marzipan holly —note intricate board work.

17. *Bottom left*—The ideal birthday cake for a girl—all pink with a "cage" of roses.

18. *Top left*—Coloured traga-canth basket decorated with royal icing loops and sugar roses and birds and used as a show piece or can be filled with dainties. The "Wedg-wood" china is pastillage.

19. *Centre left*—Edible Christmas or birthday card of pastillage.

20. *Bottom right*—Brushes and edible colouring used to paint the pastillage book and the plaque which is used as the centrepiece for the cake shown in pl. *100*.

21. *Top right*—Marzipan fruits and sugar plates and dishes—one still in the mould.

22. *Centre*—Pastillage "Peter Rabbit" plate and novelty calendars.

23. *Bottom left*—"Wedgwood" boxes and plates made of pastillage to hold homemade sweets or fruits.

24. *Top left*—A raised picture of a dog makes an attractive Christmas card while work is still in progress on a squirrel plaque.

25. *Centre right*—Pale pink and white shaded pastillage roses decorate a pale pink wedding cake.

26. *Bottom left*—Brilliant pyrethrums to decorate an Easter cake—the flowers, the dog and basket and the lettering are run-out on waxed paper and then transferred to the cake; half flowers are run-out straight on to the board.

Mixing royal icing

Having carefully prepared the bowl and utensils, put the egg white into the bowl first. Instead of pure egg white, it is possible to use a reconstituted substitute —*Hyfoama, Icine, Meriwhite*, etc., or even gelatine soaked and dissolved in water. Using a substitute solves the problem of surplus egg yolks. Gradually add the icing sugar straight from the freshly opened packet, without sieving.

It is not possible to give the correct weight of sugar to each egg, as some eggs are naturally much larger than others, some people are much more clever than others at extracting all the white from an egg, and some icing jobs need stiffer icing, and therefore more sugar, than others. However generally it may help to know that:

1 egg white will take 4 ozs. to 8 ozs. icing sugar;

or 1 teaspoon powdered substitute to ⅛ pt. cold water will take about 1 lb. sugar;

or ¼ oz. gelatine to ⅛ pt. water will take about 1 lb. sugar.

If a little yolk should get into the white when breaking an egg, it should never be used for making royal icing. It can be used for cake baking, or for family use, but another egg white must be used for the icing.

Stir or beat the white of egg and icing sugar thoroughly with a flat wooden spatula, using a vigorous stirring movement rather than actually beating. Add sugar and beat alternately until the mixture is like thick, unwhipped cream. At this stage it should pour heavily from the spoon or spatula. Continue stirring vigorously until the icing is stiff enough and will stand in a peak (pls. *12* and *13*). It may be necessary to add a little more sugar, but the more it is beaten, the stiffer the icing should become. If too much sugar is added and not enough beating done, the icing will be short, hard to pipe, and hard on the cake to cut and eat.

It is not considered possible to over-beat royal icing by hand—the accepted time is usually about twenty minutes. It is possible to take a rest half-way through,

and then to resume beating, but in the meantime, the icing should be covered with a damp cloth, wrung out in clean, cold water. A flat, wooden spatula or flat, wooden spoon should be used for beating, never a metal one, and an earthenware or porcelain bowl—again, never metal, as this causes discoloration.

If an electric food mixer is used, it should be run on a slow speed for about four minutes only, or until reaching the required stiffness. When making icing in a machine, take care to see that it is not over-beaten. This causes pockets of air, and produces fluffy icing which, if used for coating the top of a cake, will form a rough, bubbly surface instead of a smooth one, and will cause piping to break frequently because of the air in the sugar. To even up the texture of icing made by an electric machine, spend a few seconds re-beating by hand.

If an egg substitute is used in the machine, put one teaspoonful, or the required amount of powder into the pound packet of dry icing sugar, and stir together before adding to the water already in the mixer. Again, the bowl of the machine must be sterilized before making royal icing, as it will undoubtedly have been used for making cakes and creaming fat. Although a porcelain or similar bowl is better than a metal one, the metal beater used with the machine will have to be used, so make sure to scald it with boiling water. Avoid using an egg whisk, as this causes too much air to enter the icing, making it fluffy and liable to break when attempting to pipe fine lines, and liable to produce holes on a top surface, instead of a smooth, flat, close texture.

For best results, separate fresh eggs the night before making the icing, and allow the whites to stand, covered with a damp cloth.

As with everything else, perfect royal icing takes a lot of practice and a lot of patience, but the final effect is always worth the time taken. Stiff icing is suitable for stars and scroll work, a slightly softer icing for lines and writing. For covering a surface, a softer icing still (pl. *13*). If the icing is too stiff for surface work, thin it by adding a little more egg white—or water if a substitute albumen is used—and re-beating.

Obtaining a flat surface

A good, smooth, flat surface is very necessary for a cake with piping. When the almond paste on the cake has had two or three days to dry, put the cake—which should be on a silver board two inches larger than the diameter of the cake—on a turn-table, or two inverted soup plates so that the cake can easily be turned round. Re-beat the royal icing to the correct coating consistency, and test by lifting the icing on a flat wooden spoon or spatula: it should pull up in a point on the spoon, but the point should easily fall over (pl. *13*). If the icing is too stiff, it can be thinned, as explained previously, by adding a little white of egg. If it is too soft, continue beating, and only add a little more sugar if absolutely necessary.

For a seven-inch cake, place about a breakfastcupful of the royal icing in the centre of the cake, and with a palette knife, spread evenly over the surface (pl. *14*). Allow the icing to come over the sides and down to the base of the cake, using a backwards and forwards movement (pl. *15*). Wipe the knife free from icing, and then hold it at the back of the cake, with the blade across the cake tilted at an angle of 45°, the point reaching slightly beyond the centre. Place the left hand also at the back of the cake holding the cake board, and begin turning slowly, moving the blade round with the right hand, and the board with the left, so that the icing is gradually smoothed over the surface and both hands eventually meet at the front of the cake, thus completing a circle. When the entire surface is smooth, quickly lift the knife. This leaves a take-off mark which is always present when learning to coat the surface of a cake. With experience, less take-off mark will be noticeable.

When the top surface is completed, place a plastic scraper or palette knife against the side of the cake (pl. *16*)—

alternatively, use a piece of stiff, good, smooth cardboard, or smooth three-ply wood, which should be deeper than the side of the cake, and about four or five inches wide. Again, starting at the back, with both hands together, turn the cake by its base with the left hand, smoothing the icing with the scraper in the right hand, making as little take-off mark as possible. If necessary, take the scraper round the sides of the cake several times but keep it at right angles to the silver board, and resting on it, so that the cake sides are perfectly upright. Replace any "smoothed off" icing in the bowl.

An alternative method of smoothing the surface is to take the knife or a smooth steel, wooden or plastic ruler across the top of the cake (pl. *17*).

Whichever method is used, remove any surplus icing from the edge of the cake, leaving a bevelled edge—this is particularly good for piping stars.

Allow the icing to dry for two or three days in a warm place, and then with fine sandpaper, remove the take-off mark on the icing, and any other roughness on the surface. Holes which may appear can be filled with a little of the royal icing, and sandpapered smooth when dry—with more experience, this should not be necessary.

The first coat of royal icing should always be very thin as it is really only a key between the almond paste and the next coat of royal icing. Give the cake a second coat of icing in the same way as the first. Leave it in a warm place for two or three days to become quite dry, and, if necessary, use the sandpaper again to improve the surface. On special cakes, a third, or perhaps even a fourth coat of royal icing is usually necessary. Each coat gives a smoother, finer finish, but each must also be very thin, or the icing will be hard. All four coats together should not be more than one-eighth of an inch in thickness.

A good surface has beauty in itself, and does not require a lot of decorating. In fact, it is often the plainer designs that look the best, if they are neatly and well carried out. The icing should be quite firm and dry before any decorating is done, because if a mistake should occur, the icing can be far more easily removed from a dry surface than a soft one. If possible, allow the surface to dry for about a week in a warm room, before piping the decoration. When dry, keep the cake in tinfoil until ready for decorating. When decorated a box is necessary as foil would spoil the fine work. Store in a dry place—dampness will spoil icing.

To make a softer royal icing, add a teaspoonful of glycerine to each pound of icing sugar—this method, however, should never be used for exhibition or examination work, and is not advisable for wedding cakes, especially if pillars have to stand on the top surface to hold further tiers of cakes. If hard royal icing is placed in a room with a boiling kettle for a short while, the steam will make cutting easier, but even so, a good, suitable knife is necessary to cut it successfully.

It is always best to cut right across the centre of a royal iced cake, and then cut inch-wide strips. Lay the strips on a board and cut into fingers. Never attempt to cut wedge pieces, as the fine point in the centre of the cake will always crumble and fall away.

To add colour to royal icing

Royal icing will take colour well for piping or for surfacing, although it is not advisable to use sandpaper on a coloured surface, as the sugar always remains in fine grains, and sandpapering divides the grains, showing the white sugar. It is possible, of course, to sandpaper the first coat of coloured icing, and then to top with a fresh, un-sandpapered surface.

Coloured piping designs look attractive on white, but very strong colours should be used only with great care—particularly red, which is inclined to "run", especially if there is any dampness in the atmosphere.

But for the uninitiated, white icing is always the safest way to success. To make sure of producing a really good white, laundry blue is often added to white icing. Scrape only a small quantity from the block of laundry blue, and dissolve it in half a teaspoonful of cold water. When the icing is mixed, beat in the blue liquid. It may be necessary to stiffen the icing again afterwards. Be careful not to add too much blue, as it can sometimes be difficult to regain a good white; however if this does happen, keep the cake for a long time, and the icing should eventually fade to a good white again. Badly made royal icing can become yellow through under-beating, or through lack of care of utensils. As previously stressed, any grease in the icing will spoil its texture and make it run and lose its shape. More sugar is added, and a bad icing becomes worse. Not only these faults, but drying too near heat and a foggy atmosphere can also cause white icing to turn yellowish.

Laundry blue should never be added to coloured icing.

To make a Snow Scene Christmas cake as is admired in almost every confectioner's at Christmas time.

Make a firm cake with a flat top—cut to make a good surface if the cake has risen unevenly in baking. Cover carefully with marzipan or almond icing, and place on a thick silver board two inches bigger than the diameter of the cake. Allow to dry for a day or two, and then make a stiff royal icing. Half a pound of icing sugar will cover an eight-inch cake.

Put all the icing on the cake and coat the top and sides. With a dry knife, pull up the icing roughly all over to form points, and perhaps smooth one side to set flat for writing greetings.

To decorate, make a little house with marzipan. Colour a small piece of the paste red or green. Roll this out and make a roof, piping windows and doors with lines of icing. A model of Santa Claus can easily be made, and so can sprigs of holly and mistletoe (*see* Chapter Four and page 43). Make a smooth line round the middle of the side of the cake to take a gay, red ribbon.

Immediately the icing is finished, clean the board with a damp cloth to remove any icing which may have fallen on to it. This must be done at once, before the icing sets hard.

Decoration with a serrated scraper

Apart from the "snow" method, a quick and attractive surface can also be obtained by using a serrated scraper. Coat with a thin layer of royal icing as evenly as possible over the marzipan, and allow to set in a dry place for two or three days. Coat again with well-beaten icing, stiff enough to stand up in points, as for the snow scene. Using the serrated scraper, mark round the top and sides in rings or patterns (pls. *4, 56, 126*).

Fan-like patterns can be made by using the scraper with a semicircular movement, or cobweb designs by moving it convexly—variations grow as experience grows. Any take-off mark can be hidden with a decorative spray of flowers or holly.

Leave the cake to dry, and decorate the top and bottom edges with piped stars.

To obtain a perfect, flat surface

This needs an enormous amount of practice. To reach the perfection seen on professionally iced cakes is one of the most difficult jobs in cake decoration. Practice is so important that it is a good plan to make a cake model to work on. Find a suitable tin with a flat lid, about seven inches in diameter. Place the tin on a thick silver cake board or cake drum, place a small block of wood inside, and insert a screw up from under the silver board, through the tin, and into the wood. Put the lid on the tin, and practise icing it, just like a cake. As well as practising icing flat surfaces, try out designs with the serrated scraper in this way, too. The icing can be scraped off the tin when the practice is over, and kept covered with a damp cloth, in a screw-top jar or in an air-tight polythene container, until there is time to practise again, although the icing will, of course, have to be re-beaten before use.

This is the only way to become proficient. There are never enough real cakes to accommodate all the practice that every amateur cake decorator needs.

When royal icing is not in use, it should be covered with a damp cloth and kept damp all the time, to prevent the icing from drying. If it is to be kept for day-to-day practice, the cloth must be washed out daily and dried in the open air, a second cloth being used in the meantime.

The art of royal icing needs constant practice, perfect cleanliness, and a lot of attention and patience. It is the really professional icing, and there is no easy short cut to success.

CHAPTER FOUR

Modelling Cake Decorations

Modelling fruit, flowers, small figures and animals is really an art, but with experience, and by following carefully a few instructions, most people can produce good results, even if there is little of the artist in them.

Before actually beginning to model, try to find a specimen flower or fruit to copy, or even a picture, as guidance. Almond paste, marzipan and sugar paste—also known as cold fondant—are ideal materials for modelling.

ROSES

These are the most frequently seen of cake decorations, and very easily modelled. Use either a good bought almond paste, or a home-made paste of finely-milled almonds —coarsely-ground almonds are not suitable—and all icing sugar, no castor sugar, and white of egg to mix the paste. Soya flour is sometimes used in modelling paste, mixed with an equal quantity of icing sugar and white of egg. Cold fondant models well (pl. 3), but the flowers must be kept in a dry place, as they can easily lose their shape and become sticky. Pay special attention to hygiene and always wash the hands before beginning to model.

Roll out the marzipan on a practice board (*see* Chapter Five), or a wooden pastry board, lightly dredged with cornflour. For a basket of roses, one or two natural-coloured marzipan flowers can be made first, and then mixed with deeper coloured roses.

Take a piece of the marzipan to be coloured, and press a hollow in the centre. Add a few drops of colour, or a little powdered colour, and work gently until

fairly evenly mixed. At first keep the colouring quite pale, and after making a few flowers, add more colour for darker roses. Avoid over-kneading, as this makes the almond paste oily, although a little royal icing or white of egg and icing sugar can occasionally bring back the paste to the right consistency. Always keep the paste covered when not in use.

For the basic shape of the rose, make a solid cone of marzipan or sugar paste, about half an inch high and half an inch across the base (diag. 12). Roll out the remaining paste on cornflour to about one-eighth of an inch in thickness, and using a small round cocktail cutter, cut a small circle about the size of a sixpence. The size of the cutter and thickness of the paste will determine the size of the rose petal. Do not cut more than two or three circles at a time, as the edges dry and make cracked petals. Cover the marzipan on the board with a slightly damp cloth while working the petals.

Hold the edge of one of the small circles in the left hand, dust the fingers of the other hand with a very little cornflour, and proceed to press the rest of the circle of marzipan until it is as thin as paper. Held up to the light it should be possible to see daylight through it. The piece of the circle between the left thumb and finger should be kept thick, as this helps to build up the heart of the rose. Wrap this thin petal round the cone, completely enclosing it (diag. 13). The base of the petal—that is, the thick part—should be dampened with a little white of egg or water, using a small paint brush or the back of a teaspoon.

Thin out a second petal, keeping the thick base in the left thumb and finger, and dipping the right thumb and finger in a little cornflour. Moisten the base and place this petal behind the first closed one, curling it back slightly.

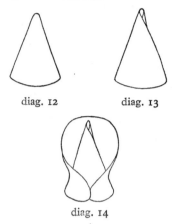

diag. 12   diag. 13

diag. 14

Continue making petals and placing in position, curling each one back a little more. Three petals are usually sufficient to encircle the first closed one. For a small rose, four petals in all are enough, but individual judgement should be relied upon to continue adding petals until the rose looks finished. To curve the outer petals, shape the circle of marzipan in the hollow of the hand, or even over a hard-boiled egg.

To make a shaded rose, press together a circle of yellow marzipan, and a circle of pink. Cut to the right size, and continue pressing to complete the petal.

Again, this is an art, and requires plenty of practice and patience in order to know how to place the petals for the best effect. Avoid pressing the rose centre into a long shape or it may lose its form and begin to resemble a cabbage. Also avoid putting too many petals on a rose. To make a bigger rose it is better to use a larger circle of paste than extra petals. If the base of the rose does become long, cut off a little with a knife or scissors before leaving it to dry. Any left-over marzipan should be wrapped in waxed paper and stored in a screw-top jar—even small pieces come in useful for modelling two or three tiny flowers, berries or fruits.

Have an egg box ready for the completed flowers, each part lined with a little grease-proof paper. Place the roses separately in each compartment to keep them from breaking.

To give a realistic finish to a rose, dust it with a little carmine powder. Insert a piece of rustless wire in the base of the rose by heating the wire till very hot and then pushing it in position. This melts the sugar, which soon cools again and sets, fastening the rose to the wire. Place in a dry room for a while to harden the rose, then hold it over a pan of boiling water to coat with steam. Have ready some carmine powder on greaseproof paper. Hold the steamed rose over the paper and dust the powder onto the petals, using a fine sable brush. Shake gently to remove any surplus, and return any dry powder to the bottle. Cover the wire with green marzipan, as a stem.

Always take the greatest care with carmine powder. It stains easily, and the slightest draught will blow it around. Always wear an overall, and only use the powder for very special work. Never use cold fondant for carmine-powdered roses, as it is not suitable for holding a stem. For the basket-of-roses cake it is not necessary to put a wire stem on the rose.

FRUITS

Marzipan fruits can be used either as a decoration on a cake, as sweetmeats, or for serving as *petits fours* after a meal. As a decoration on a cake, they should be much smaller than for *petits fours* or sweets. Small pieces of left-over marzipan can be modelled into different fruits for cake decoration and kept in an air-tight container to prevent them from becoming hard.

Apples

Use natural-coloured, good quality or home-made marzipan. After washing the hands—marzipan easily picks up any dust and becomes soiled—roll a small ball of marzipan. Make a slight indentation in the top and base of the apple. Using some red colouring diluted with water, and a fine artist's paint brush, colour the marzipan apple realistically on one side, blending the colour to a paler shade. Similarly, paint the other side green, blending the red and green slightly, rubbing in the colours until they merge gently. Using scissors, cut a clove in two, and place one piece in the apple as the stem, and the other as the calyx.

Place the finished apples with other marzipan fruits in paper cases in an attractive box (pl. 4), or add a few leaves modelled in green marzipan, and use the fruits to decorate a cake.

Pears

Make these similarly to apples. Begin with a suitably sized ball, about three-quarters of an inch across, bringing up one side to a pear shape by working it round in the fingers. Use the same method of colouring as for apples.

Bananas

Use a long, square, ridged shape, painted with edible colour in yellow and green with touches of brown. Very realistic and unusual.

Oranges and lemons

Form a good shape first, and then mark the outside with a pin head or roll on a grater to form the texture of the surface peel. Colour orange and yellow.

Strawberries

After shaping and colouring, roll in granulated sugar to give the seed effect. A green hull can be made from marzipan.

Peaches

Shape and colour, and mark a line on one side with a knife.

Vegetables

Cauliflowers, cabbages, carrots, turnips —each one can be copied and makes a novel decoration.

Houses

Make a small oblong of marzipan about one-and-a-quarter inches long by three-quarters of an inch wide. Build up to a pointed ridge. Colour some marzipan green or red and roll out an oblong to cover the ridge. Represent tiles by marking lines with a knife. Fix the roof to the house with jam. Pipe tiny doors and windows. With experience, even quite elaborate Norwegian houses can be modelled.

Holly

Colour a little marzipan red and roll into tiny berries the size of a lentil. Colour the remainder of the paste green, but do not attempt to make the marzipan dark-green like real holly. Roll out the green marzipan very thinly on a board lightly dredged with cornflour, and cut into strips a quarter of an inch wide. Cut off the end of the strip like ribbon cut on the cross. Continue cutting diagonally down the strip, producing several diamond shapes (diag. 15).

Put the first finger of the left hand on top of one of these diamond shapes, and with a skewer, push in the point on one side of the diamond. Push in also above and below the point. Repeat on the other side (diag. 16). Repeat pushing on the first side if necessary. Mark the centre with a knife to represent the vein of the leaf. A number one or two icing tube may also be used as a cutter to produce the shape of the holly leaf instead of the "pushing" method.

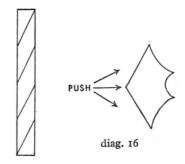

PUSH

diag. 16

diag. 15

When the leaves and berries are dry, store them in a tin, and at Christmas-time arrange them on a chocolate yule log or a cake with a few marzipan stems (pls. *9* and *24*). A tiny dab of water from an artist's paint brush can be used to moisten the leaves and berries to fix them in position. Ivy leaves and mistletoe can be made in the same way, using the natural coloured marzipan for berries.

BIRDS' NESTS
(to decorate a simnel cake)

Shape a small piece of almond paste into a ball, hollowing out the centre and pressing into the shape of a bird's nest. Colour some royal icing straw colour or brown, and with a number one tube, pipe strands of icing over the nest and round the edges. Make several tiny marzipan eggs, colour some blue, and perhaps some spotted, and place them in the nest. Model a bird—chicken, robin, thrush, etc.—or buy a yellow cottonwool chick.

These nests are most generally used to decorate a simnel cake, but for an even more unusual effect, make some small round cakes in bun tins, and place one of these nests on each cake. This makes a different and very popular Easter novelty.

SPRING FLOWERS

Use good quality marzipan, coloured yellow. Roll out thinly with a rolling-pin, using cornflour on the board. With a natural flower, or a good picture as a guide, cut a strip suitable for the width of a daffodil trumpet. Mould this round the fingers, and work in the join until it disappears. For each flower, cut six petal shapes with a knife. Shape and press thinly at the edges. Arrange in position on wax paper, using folded tissue paper to lift the petals slightly to form a natural shape. Moisten the base of the trumpet and set it in position. Prop with tissue-paper until firm.

ANIMALS

For these, the paste must be just right in consistency, neither too dry, nor too soft. If it is dry, add a little glucose or glycerine, If soft, add a little icing sugar.

To make a rabbit, form the marzipan into a roll about a finger's thickness. Cut off a piece and form into an oval for the head. Shape into a cone with a point at

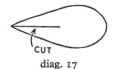

diag. 17

one end, and cut down the point with scissors to make the rabbit's ears (diag. 17). Bend under one end of the marzipan roll and curve round to form the body and back legs. With scissors, cut the other end of the roll to form two front legs (diag. 18).

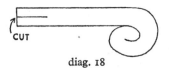

diag. 18

Complete the shaping with fingers and thumb, and fix the head in position with a little white of egg. When set firm, make a dot of white royal icing for the eye, and centre each dot with a tiny blob of chocolate icing (diag. 19).

diag. 19

Pigs, mice, chickens and birds can be made in the same way (pl. **6**). They are all especially popular at children's parties. Colour the animals using a fine artist's brush and edible colour.

From these basic instructions, almost any idea can be achieved for Christmas (pl. **7**), birthday, or any special occasion.

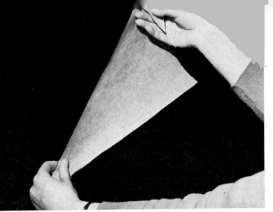

18. *Step 1:* hold triangle of paper with short side at top and long side on left. Bring together points each end of short side.

19. *Step 2:* bring bottom point round to top point in right hand to form a cone.

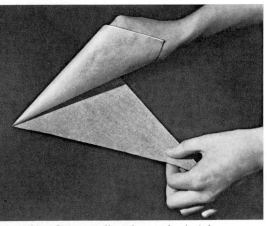

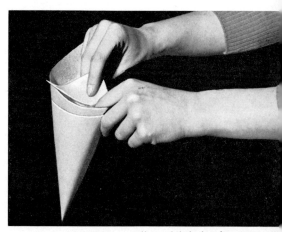

20. *Step 3:* pull up long point in left hand until all three points are more or less together.

21. *Step 4:* pull up tightly leaving no hole at point of cone. Fold in top flap twice to secure. Fill bag with icing and cut off tip to give size of hole required.

22. *Step 5:* fold bag to give flat cushion top for thumb. Hold bag with fingers at side and press with thumb only. Steady with left hand.

23. *Step 6:* to use a double-sized bag for large, heavy work, pressure comes from fingers and palm of hand, bag kept closed with the thumb.

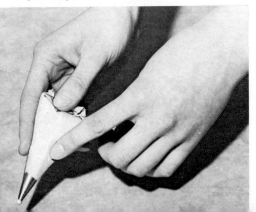

24. *Left*—Holly and candle modelled from marzipan—the ideal decoration for a Christmas cake.

25. *Below*—Cake decorated with an eight point star design of interlacing lines—these may be extended to cover the entire surface.

26. *Below*—Making a feather design: (1) piping chocolate lines on to a glacé iced cake; (2) draw knife across while still wet; (3) the finished cake.

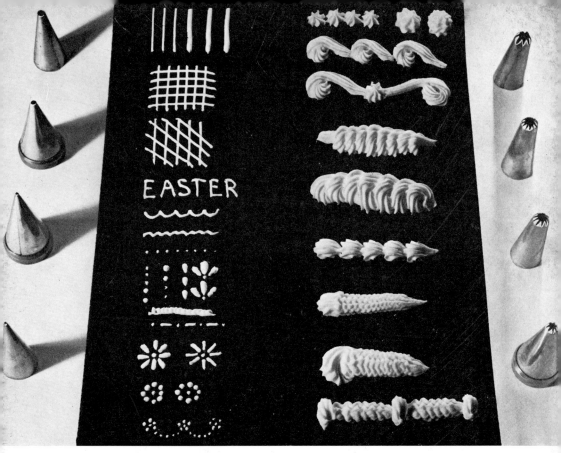

EASTER

27. Icing tubes: *left hand*—writing tubes one to four and work that can be done with them; *right hand*—star tubes, the most useful, number five at the bottom.

28. A tennis cake using run-out figures and the 'quilting' pattern with pink roses and green leaves at each intersection.

29. *Above*—The eight point star pattern piped on to a royal iced cake—to make template see diagrams 36 and 37.

30. *Above*—A concave design using trellis and shells to accentuate effect—to make template see diagrams 38 and 39.

31. *Left*—Convex eight point pattern built up four times on the outer line—to make template see diagrams 40 and 41. Snowmen made in pastillage.

32. *Right*—Initial-centred cake suitable for a man's birthday—to make template see diagrams 46 & 49 and 48 & 49 for the centre.

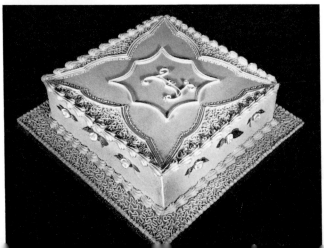

CHAPTER FIVE

Learning to Pipe Designs

Piping is a fascinating art. The simplest designs can be easily executed, and the most intricate designs can be carried out from the instructions given. But to achieve any worthwhile result, as with all else in the art of cake decorating, there is only one road to success: practice.

Because practice is so all-important, it is best to provide ample facilities for practising before attempting to begin to learn piping. As a model cake-surface helped in practising to ice a smooth surface, so a practice board will help towards practising piped designs.

Making a practice board

Cover a thick silver cake board or cake drum with one of the many kinds of self-adhesive plastic coverings similar to those used on sink drainers or shelves. If the bottom of the board is covered with a plastic covering—plain colours, yellow, brown or blue, are best—the silver side can still be used as a cake board. Patterned surfaces are difficult to pipe onto without straining the eyes. If old boards do become untidy, the silver paper for re-covering them can be bought cheaply from Messrs. F. G. Kettle, 127 High Holborn, W.C.1. This is obtainable to personal shoppers only, and is not sent by post.

Once the practice board is made, keep it for trying out designs before working on the actual cake, and for practising the balance of a proposed design, and the arrangement of lettering and sugar flower sprays.

Making a piping bag

Paper bags made by hand with greaseproof paper are usually far the best for royal icing. Metal icing sets or pumps are available, but are difficult to use. Icing bags made of calico are apt to make the

hands sticky, and plastic or nylon bags require careful washing. On the whole, paper icing bags are less wasteful and far less trouble, as they can simply be burned after use.

Using the best quality greaseproof paper —sheets usually measure about thirty inches by twenty inches—fold one sheet in half, then in half again and again. Open out. The sheet is now divided into eight oblongs, all ten inches by seven and a half inches (diag. 20). Cut out these oblongs and cut each one across diagonally, from corner to corner, making sixteen triangles of paper, sufficient for sixteen icing bags, with no waste of greaseproof (diag. 21).

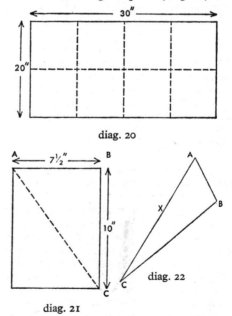

diag. 20

diag. 21

diag. 22

To make the greaseproof bags, hold one of the paper triangles with the longest side on the left, and the shortest side at the top (diag. 22). With the right hand, in the paper, take hold of point A. Bring point A to point B and take point C forward and then round the back to meet A and B, forming a cone with the point at X. There should be no hole at the point X, and X should be a sharp point. If there is any hole at X, adjust carefully, pulling the long point of paper. Make the bag secure by folding in the long point. Plates *18* to *23* show the making of these bags in detail.

Only make enough bags for immediate use, as storing can flatten and crease the points.

Filling the bags with icing

For practice work, about half an egg white can be kept aside from the general daily cookery, and saved in a screw-top jar or covered with a damp cloth. To the egg white add enough icing sugar to make a stiff icing when well beaten—stiff enough to pull up into peaks.

Hold the bag in the left hand with the thumb on the outside. Take up some of the royal icing on a thin kitchen knife, not a wide palette knife, draw the icing in a long point, and place the point of icing down into the bag. Bring the knife against the left thumb, pressing the icing off the knife. Do not press the bag together, as a second amount of icing may have to be put into the bag, and even a third if necessary. Take care not to over-fill the bag, as this can cause the icing to come out at the top, or the bag to burst. Fold over the bag carefully at the top and press the icing down towards the point. Then fold the sides down on the top to give a flat, cushion-like rest for the thumb.

Before beginning to pipe, it will be necessary to cut the point off the bag to make a small hole—only use metal nozzles after some practice with the paper icing bag alone. For fine line work, cut about one-sixteenth of an inch from the bag. It is important to make this cut at right angles to the bag, and not on the slant. This cut should give a hole equal to the number one writing tube.

From now on, the basin of icing must be kept covered with a wet cloth. If the paper cone is carefully unfolded, any icing from a finished bag can be scraped back into the bowl. Re-beat before filling each bag. Avoid the temptation to eat the icing. Special care must be paid to hygiene, and finger-licking must not be allowed. Keep a damp sponge ready for wiping the hands.

To begin piping

A beginner should start by practising straight lines onto the practice board or the back of a plate. Hold the paper icing bag with the fingers at the side, and press with the thumb only on the flat, folded paper cushion at the top. Practise for some time before attempting to work on a cake. In fact, however proficient, it is always a good idea to try out the size of the hole cut in the piping bag before beginning to work on a cake.

With the point of the bag just touching the plate or practice board, press gently with the thumb. Watch the work carefully all the time. Move on as soon as the icing starts to come from the tube, making a smooth line. If a knob occurs, it is either because the icing is being pressed from the bag before it is in contact with the practice board, or else the movement is not quick enough. The beginner will soon learn to regulate the pressure on the icing bag and to balance the rate of movement, so that just enough icing is pressed out to make the line even.

It is also important to finish without a knob. When the end of the line of icing is nearly reached, release the thumb pressure and lay down the icing, touching the board to break it off.

If the finished line is wavy, the pressure has been too great. If the line breaks, the pressure has been too little. To become expert, continue making lines until perfect. If the line twists, raise the tube or bag more. The line of piping coming from the bag should always be about half an inch to an inch above the practice board. Do not be afraid to lift the work—a straighter line will be obtained this way, and any twists in the icing line will have time to straighten out before it is laid down on the design. It is not lifting that breaks a line, but insufficient pressure. The student should pipe towards herself whenever possible, never backwards.

As a change from making straight lines, try writing, and making a row of dots. This is good practice for starting and stopping. To make dots, touch the board and raise quickly, using hardly any pressure. When writing, lift the line of piping and allow the icing to run from the bag. Do not try to keep the bag on the board all the time.

After really thorough practice with the paper bag only, try using a metal tube. A number one plain tube is suitable for lines and gives a continued, even line, whereas the bag eventually wears out at the point, and cannot make an even thickness of line for any length of time.

Cut off about half an inch of paper from the end of the bag, and insert the tube. Make sure it comes through the hole sufficiently as the end of the paper bag can interfere with the shape of the icing, particularly when using a star tube (pls. *22* and *23*). To fill the bag, hold it in the left hand, as before, but take extra care not to allow the icing to escape between the tube and the bag by disturbing the close fit of the tube.

Never press onto the practice board so hard that the tube is pushed back into the bag. This would allow the icing to seep down between the bag and the tube, and present enormous difficulties. Apart from this hazard, piping lines with a metal tube is much the same as piping with the bag alone.

For more practice, try making dots with the writing tube—by pushing out more icing, a bigger dot is formed. Make graduated dots, remembering all the time to hold the bag at right angles above the board. Press gently, giving only one squeeze. Stop pressing and raise the bag quickly. Gradually increase the size of the dot by exerting greater pressure on the bag and raising it quickly.

Using the star tube

A **star tube** number five is useful to have, although bigger star tubes with the same number or more points, are needed for more advanced work.

Making stars is almost the same as making dots. Make a new paper icing bag, and insert a star tube. Use very stiff icing to avoid a point—a good star should be made without a point. Hold the tube at right angles to the cake or board, almost touching it, and press out some icing. Raise the tube quickly. Practise making large or small stars, all with the same tube, by pressing out more or less icing.

Vary the practice by buying small shilling-sized biscuits, or making them with a cocktail cutter, and icing each one with a star. This makes a good practice exercise and is interesting as well—especially if the icing is coloured with a few drops of edible colouring. These small star biscuits are perfect for a children's party. Alternatively, for a cocktail party, beat up some soft cream cheese and pipe stars onto savoury biscuits. Sprinkle with chopped parsley.

Building up a design

Using a number one icing tube, or a bag cut to the same size, work out the following design for a round cake. Make two tiny dots of icing opposite each other at the highest and lowest points on the edge of a round practice board. Turn the board a quarter-circle, and make a third and fourth dot at the points now highest and lowest on the circle. Make four more dots between those already made, marking eight equal spaces. Now make a second row of dots, one inch in from the edge of the board, and half-way between each of the previous dots, as in diagram 23. Make icing lines joining the dots, as in diagram 24, to form an eight-point star. Complete the design with several more lines to form three eight-point stars inside each other and a row of dots as in diagram 25.

To give the professional finish to this design, build it up by working a second line of piping on the middle star, and a second and third line of piping exactly on top of each other, on the outer star. Graduated dots give the finishing touch of interest to the design (pl. **8**). On the cake used for this actual photograph, pink glacé icing formed the surface, the eight-

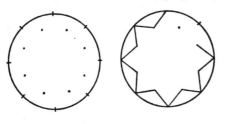

diag. 23   diag. 24

diag. 25

point star design being carried out in white royal icing. A great deal of practice is needed to put these lines perfectly on top of one another.

In the following diagrams, variations of the eight-point star pattern are shown. The marking dots are the same in each case, but the line work on each one gives a different design. These should all be practised as an exercise, and when perfected, can be piped in royal icing onto a sponge sandwich cake with a flat top, previously iced with glacé icing and allowed to become quite set. Pale-coloured glacé icing with white royal piping, or white glacé and coloured piping look equally attractive. Left-over glacé icing can be used for piping by adding a small quantity of powdered albumen egg substitute, and beating well to a suitable stiffness and texture to serve as a home purpose royal icing. This type of cake, with this type of decoration, should be made and eaten the same day, as glacé icing softens the royal icing. Nevertheless, this is all good practice, and piping designs onto a

cake often inspires far more interest, effort and enthusiasm than simply piping onto a practice board.

For further practice, try experimenting with more line designs—the wider the range of practice designs, the more interest will be held. With royal icing, make a straight line through the centre of the cake, from top to bottom. Turn the cake a quarter circle to the left, and make a second line from top to bottom, dividing the cake into quarters. Again turning the cake to the left, make a third line a quarter of an inch to the right of the first line. Turn to the left again, and work a fourth line, on the right of the second line, and a quarter of an inch from it. Continue making these lines a quarter of an inch apart, always turning the cake to the left, and always piping the new line on the right of the existing lines, until the whole cake is covered. The result should be an intriguing, interlacing square pattern.

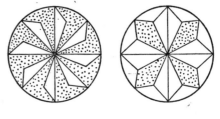

diag. 26   diag. 27

diag. 28

If preferred, two colours can be used, in two tubes of the same thickness. Using pink, or blue, and white, keep the pink lines running next to each other, and the white lines running parallel to each other. Even three or four interlacing lines make a simple and attractive design on a glacé-iced cake. It is not necessary to keep the lines central (diag. 29), and a small decoration, perhaps a cherry, a nut, or some simple lettering, can fill the quarter space.

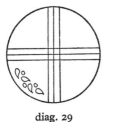

diag. 29

After some practice, a cake can be turned one-sixth, or one-eighth, and the lines crossed in the same way, producing a six- or eight-point star of interlacing lines, which is fascinating to work, and gives a most attractive finish (pl. 25).

Using a star tube for scrolls

Star tubes vary from a number five tube, to a number fifteen. A larger star can be made with a small tube simply by pressing more icing from the bag, but a small star cannot be made with a larger tube. Bearing this in mind, buy the smaller tubes at first. Of these small star tubes, a number five is perhaps the most useful. It has eight points, and makes a neat star (pl. 27).

To make a scroll, use the number five star tube, and holding it as if making a star, move along in the lines of a sideways question mark. The tail end of the scroll should be thinned out as it is finished, and the head of the question mark should be almost closed. Work left-hand and right-hand scrolls, bringing the points together and neatening with a star (pl. 27). When proficient use the star tube to edge cakes with stars or scrolls.

For variations, outline scrolls on a practice board with fine lines or dots, or over-pipe by building up lines on the scroll with a number one tube. Improve on old ideas or search out new ones by looking at the photographs in this book, at the cakes in shop windows, and even by studying the scroll work on the ceilings in old houses and halls.

Metal icing tubes or nozzles may be bought from Messrs. G. F. & H. J. Mathews & Co. Ltd., 214 Borough High Street, London SE1.

CHAPTER SIX

Piping Decorations

Some of the most fascinating cakes to ice, and also those which give the most pleasure, are cakes with individual or topical designs and scenes. With patience and practice it is possible to produce the most intricate and specific scenes—a game of tennis for the twenty-first birthday cake of a sport enthusiast; a garden; a sea-gull scene or a Christmas scene for children.

Begin by learning to make birds for decoration. These are perhaps the simplest of all figures to make, and can be used on almost any type of cake, even an ornate wedding cake.

Icing for piping birds should be slightly softer than for piping lines or stars, and a paper bag is preferable to an icing tube, as this gives a softer line. Make a neat, firm bag, fill with well-beaten icing, and fold down tidily, as it is necessary to have full control.

In the beginning, as a rough guide, draw a pattern of the wings on greaseproof paper (diag. 30), using a coin to make a good curve. Cover the greaseproof with thin waxed paper so that the pattern can still be seen clearly. Cut the paper icing bag to the size of a number one tube and work curved lines onto the waxed paper, beginning at point A and working backwards and forwards between A and B without lifting the tube, until the entire wing span is filled (diag. 31). Each line must be shorter than the previous one, and all must be touching each other or the wing will break. The inner edge must be straight, to insert into the bird's body, and the icing should resemble feathers.

Make the wings in pairs, left and right, and to each pair of wings, make a tail, either straight or fan-tailed according to the species of bird (diag. 32).

Leave the wings and tails until quite

dry, and then remove them very carefully from the waxed paper. Until they are needed, keep in a box cradled in cotton wadding.

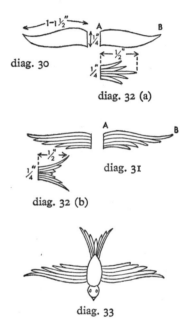

diag. 30

diag. 32 (a)

diag. 31

diag. 32 (b)

diag. 33

To make a bird's body, use a well-beaten, stiff icing, and cut off the end of the icing bag to equal a number four plain tube. Touch the waxed paper and press out a bulb of icing, keeping the point of the bag in one place all the time. When the bulb is slightly more than a quarter of an inch long, raise the bag a little to form the neck, and press again to form the head. Pull off very quickly to make the beak. Only the well-shaped bodies should be used.

When a good body has been made, insert one of the dry sugar tails, in the

54

correct position, and a left and right wing, taking care that the curve done first—A to B—is at the head of the bird, otherwise the wings will be flying one way, and the body another!

When each bird is made, use a tiny piece of crushed tissue-paper to prop up the tail and wings, and when quite dry, paint the beak yellow or orange with edible colouring, and add two dark dots for eyes, using a very fine artists' brush (diag. 33). Store in a box with wadding till required, still on the waxed paper. When proficient the body can be made straight onto the cake and the dry wings and tail inserted. The body only can be made in yellow icing to represent ducks.

Designing a sea-gull scene (pl. **8**)

Most suitable for this type of icing scene, is a Madeira type plain cake or a sponge sandwich. Spread the sides of the cake with a little glacé icing, and roll in toasted almonds or coconut, and place the cake on a doyley on the plate, ready for serving.

Make some glacé icing, using about one ounce of sugar to an inch of the diameter of the cake. Colour the icing pale-blue, and coat the entire top of the cake, just to the edge. Leave to set. Using a bag only, or a number one tube, pipe wavy lines of white royal icing across one-third of the cake, to represent the sea. Add a freehand lighthouse, clouds, flying birds, and, if the cake surface is large enough, a yacht. This is essentially a quick cake, so only the outlines are necessary simply to convey the idea, rather than a full-scale intricate, artistic picture. When the rest of the scene is set, place the sugar birds already made in position on the waves. When making this scene for the first time, try out on the practice board.

If necessary, the cake can be neatened round the edge, using the bag cut with a large hole for the birds' bodies. Pipe round bulbs of white royal icing about the size of a pea, touching each other all round the edge of the cake. Allow to dry, and finally add a little of the powdered albumen substitute to the blue icing that

is left, beat well, and using a number one tube join two of the bulbs by over-piping a letter S round every two bulbs of icing. This must be neatly done, and gives good practice in over-piping, constantly needed in later work.

Piping birds onto a cake surface

Sometimes flying birds have to be piped side-view onto the side of a cake, and it is impossible to make both wings and the tail on waxed paper first. In this case, pipe one wing onto the waxed paper and leave it to dry. Pipe the second wing straight onto the cake in the right position, and using another bag with a large hole, pipe the body and head of the bird as described previously, but sideways, bringing off the beak near the cake. Reverting to the finer bag, pipe in the tail and then insert the other wing, which should be quite dry. If the body icing is firm but not dry, the wing should stay well in position. Paint in the beak and eye with edible colour.

With more experience it is possible to shade the birds, using dark and light greys to give reality to the gulls' wings.

These basic ideas can be used for making most other species. Colour the icing black to make blackbirds, blue for bluebirds, or brown for sparrows. To make a robin, pipe a little red icing onto the breast of a brown bird. All these can be practised and improved upon, and eventually stored in a dry, safe place for future use.

Designing a garden scene

This is the perfect design for a small tea-party. It should be used on a Victoria sandwich, or Madeira or Genoese cake, and it should be eaten the same day it is made, as these decorations will not keep well.

Before beginning to ice the top of the cake, coat the sides with toasted nut or chocolate vermicelli, and place ready on a plate with a doyley. Ice to an indefinite line half-way across the top surface of the cake with pale-blue glacé icing. About a quarter of a pound of icing sugar will be needed for an eight-inch cake. Add a little more icing sugar to the basin—again about a quarter of a pound—and colour pale-green. Ice the remaining lower half of the cake with this green icing, coaxing it to meet the pale-blue. Leave to dry. Keep the green icing soft by putting a damp cloth over the basin.

When this surface is set, make brown icing by adding cocoa to the remaining green icing, and mix to the right consistency for piping by adding a little more water or cocoa. Pipe a line representing a road, running along the join of the green and blue icing. Add a second line on the green icing, to form a converging road. Quite simply pipe a house, freehand, and make any tree trunks, crazy paving, or fences, and perhaps a small sundial (diag. 34). Make clouds with white royal icing, and a few daisies in the green grass, using tiny lines for petals. Colour a little icing pink or yellow, and pipe more flowers into the garden, using tiny dots for delphiniums and hollyhocks, and adding

diag. 34

roses round the house and a little green icing to complete the trees. The effect should be quite realistic. If necessary, copy a picture, including archways, gates, or even being more ambitious and outlining the house first, and then filling in just to the piping line. The sundial and flowers can be made on waxed paper before placing in position, but most intricate work is preferable on a royal iced cake, as it will keep far longer. As a final touch, add some tiny brown birds to the scene.

Feather icing (pl. 26)

This design always has a professional effect, but is actually very easy to carry out.

A Victoria sandwich is the most suitable basis, and the work should be done quickly before the icing has time to set.

As always, complete the sides of the cake, and place with a doyley on a plate. Before beginning to ice, make sure that all the ingredients and utensils are ready to hand: icing sugar, cocoa or instant coffee, hot water, greaseproof paper, icing bag, palette knife and skewer. Ice the top of the cake with white glacé icing just thick enough to flow easily without running down the sides of the cake. Quickly add a little cocoa or instant coffee to the remaining icing, and, if necessary, a little warm water. Put this into the ready-made icing bag.

Cut off the point of the bag, and ice straight lines half an inch apart, across the whole of the top of the cake, beginning in the middle so that it is easier to pipe the lines parallel. Immediately the lines are completed, draw a skewer or knife point across them at right angles, again beginning in the middle. These skewer lines should be three-quarters of an inch apart. Turn the cake round, and draw the skewer across again in between each of the first skewer lines. Each step is shown clearly in plate *26*.

Allow the icing to set, and neaten with a star tube, using butter cream or Vienna icing. The stars or scrolls should be close together and placed on the edge of the cake, using the tube at right angles to the edge. Press out the right size star, and break off sharply. A second row of stars round the base of a cake gives a neat finish, and allows the cake to "sit" nicely on the dish.

A variety of patterns can be made using this basic method, and not only chocolate and coffee icings, but coloured icings give an attractive pastel effect.

Designing a tennis cake (pl. *28*)

This is definitely a novelty cake, enormously popular at a tennis party tea, or as a birthday cake for a keen tennis player.

Bake a Madeira, light cherry, sultana, or coconut cake in a loaf tin with sloping

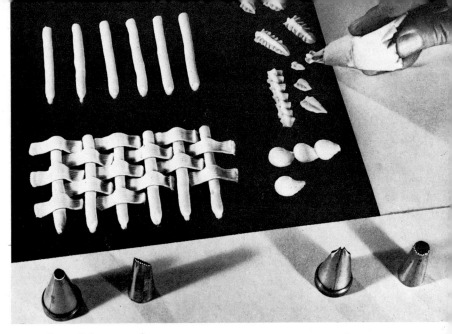

33. Above—Demonstration of leaves and cockleshells and of weaving, stakes made with number four tube and woven across with number twenty-three ribbon tube.

34. Right—Basket cake using divided lid and handle made of royal icing using a ribbon tube over cardboard or wire.

35. Bottom left—Engagement cake using variation on square template: using diagram 46, add a point and one small and one larger semi-circle at the corner.

36. Bottom right—Christmas cake using template for side loops and braiding for decoration.

37. Square basket of roses cake with pastillage padlock and key.

38. *Above*—Round basket cake decorated with a ribbon bow to match the roses modelled in marzipan.

39. *Left*—The practice board in use showing sweet peas, pansies, a flat five-petal flower, bunches of grapes and snowdrops.

40. *Below*—An Easter cake decorated with daffodils and maidenhair fern and a box containing a spray of narcissi on fern. Lettering is stencilled onto this cake.

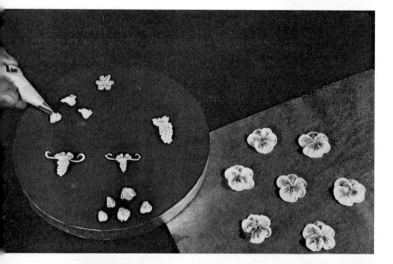

42. Icing sprinkled with yellow castor sugar makes a simple mimosa decoration.

41. *Above*—An elaborate cake using royal icing to pipe daffodils, narcissi and bunches of violets in baskets.

43. *Right*—Easter novelty cradle made from two halves of a chocolate egg, and gift box of piped sugar pansies and green leaves decorated with fern.

44. *Below*—Chocolate Easter egg decorated with pastillage butterfly and piped sugar flowers—the orchid can also be made from pastillage.

45. Preparation of chocolate boxes: square cut from chocolate melted on to waxed paper and the completed boxes, finished with a piped star of butter or dairy cream.

46. Chocolate torton, finished with a bow of golden cord.

47. Gateau for a games party.

48. *Top right*—Small chocolate Easter eggs decorated with royal icing and set in a sponge cake piped with butter cream and centred with coconut.

49. *Centre Left*—Gateau with fruit set in quick setting jelly, edged with cream and decorated with piped chocolate rabbits and ducks. Cream stars are piped sideways to form the ducks' bodies.

50. *Centre right*—Box made from marzipan covered with icing stakes and weaving, formed round a tin covered with waxed paper. The box is filled with small Easter eggs and decorated with sugar flowers.

51. *Bottom right*—Special occasion cake decorated with large chocolate heart shape. Make chocolate heart on waxed paper using template, and pipe in decoration when cold, set on thick layer of cream and roses and neaten with piping down centre.

52. *Above*—Biscuit patterns possible with chocolate or coloured icing.

53. *Right*—Lace heart shapes being piped on to waxed paper ready to put on to bicuits already iced with pale coloured glacé icing.

54. *Bottom right*—Children's engine cake made from two chocolate swiss rolls.

55. *Bottom left*—Gateau decorated with butter cream from a star tube and piped chocolate hearts; half picture of another gateau decorated with butter cream in a serrated scraper pattern and piped chocolate shapes.

56. *Right*—Elaborate gateau using thick butter cream, piped flowers and chocolate scrolls.

57. *Centre left*—Crinoline lady cake decorated with butter cream.

58. *Bottom left*—Chocolate butter cream gateau, the centre marked first with a biscuit cutter and chocolate triangles placed on eight lines of stars.

59. *Above*—Wedding cake using domed and boat-shaped raised lace work.

60. *Above*—A pink raised lace dome hides a slipper on a silver wedding cake. The dome is edged with silver leaves and pink roses.

61. *Above*—Birthday cake with a donkey and trellis cart filled with piped flowers on green iced wire stems. The trellis can be worked on a mould or in sections on waxed paper and fixed together.

62. *Left*—Lace work ornaments.

63. *Right*—Cake decorated with zig-zag lace work triangles. Angels are modelled in cold fondant and hold wax candles.

sides. Hollow out the centre of the mixture before baking to try to obtain a level surface when the cake is baked. If this is not successful, cut the top of the cake level, and turn the cake upside down. Coat the sides with pale-green icing and dip in pale-green coconut. Place ready for icing on a silver board or on a doyley on a plate, and try to avoid moving after icing. Use pale-green icing for the top surface.

Measure the sides of the cake, and draw this size onto a piece of paper. Mark out the lines of a tennis court, leaving about an inch each end, and half an inch spare on the sides of the paper. When the correct basic idea has been planned out and is well in mind, pipe the lines onto the cake in white royal icing. "Dye" a little strip of butter muslin in some of the green edible colouring, iron it out, cut to the correct size for a net, and attach each end to a cocktail stick with royal icing. Place this across the lines of the tennis court in the correct position. Pipe a line of white icing along the top of the net.

Small plastic dolls can be used for figures, or use the instructions later in this book, for making run-out figures (see Chapter Fourteen). Pipe tennis rackets lying on the grass, and perhaps a few balls on the court, made with a large dot of soft royal icing.

Making the quilting pattern (pl. *28*)

Cover a cake with royal icing over almond paste or water icing, to make a good surface. If the top surface is covered with water icing, the sides should be coated with nut. Using a number one tube and white royal icing, pipe a line across the centre of the cake. Continue piping lines parallel to this central line, and one inch apart. Now turn the cake through one-eighth of a circle to the left and again make a line through the centre, crossing the first line at an angle of about 45°. Make parallel lines, again one inch apart so that a diamond pattern is formed.

To complete the design, make small green leaves at each intersection, and add little pink rosebuds by working a tiny circle of pink royal icing between each leaf.

Designing a music cake

Use an oblong Madeira or light fruit cake, and cover the surface with cold fondant or glacé icing, first covering the sides with nuts. Pipe lines in chocolate icing and put in the music notes of the score, copying from an authentic but simple piece of music. This makes a novel decoration for a musical party, and is quite simple to carry out.

Use five lines and "one finger" music of *Happy Birthday To You* as a delightful design for a birthday cake (diag. 35). *See also* plate *183*.

diag. 35

CHAPTER SEVEN

Piping Designs for Royal Iced Cakes

As experience is gained, more elaborate designs can be attempted, and these invariably need a certain amount of planning. All intricate piping patterns must first be worked out carefully before the design is carried out on the actual cake —for this purpose, it is useful to make several cardboard templates. This chapter deals with a few of the methods of producing a variety of accurate, complicated designs.

Before beginning to pipe a design, always make sure of a good surface by giving a cake two, three, or even more good coats of royal icing.

Planning patterns for a round cake

It is possible to buy a set of marking rings (pl. *10*) or to make similar rings in cardboard, to help produce correct designs and evenly-spaced patterns. An equally good and sometimes simpler method is to cut a piece of greaseproof paper to the same size as the top of the cake using the cake baking tin as a guide. For patterns with eight points, fold this paper in half, in half again, and in half again, each time from the centre point. Keeping the paper folded, carefully fold once more, and with a soft pencil mark a straight line, as in diagram 36 from A to B.

Cut through this line and open out. The paper should now be in the shape of an eight-point star (diag. 37). This provides a good basis for a variety of designs (pl. *29*).

Designing curved patterns

Again, cut paper to the exact size of the cake top—it is helpful when doing this to use the baking tin as a guide. Fold in the same way as described previously for an eight-point star, and mark with a pencil in a concave or a convex curve. Cut through the line to achieve the appropriate pattern (diags. 38–41). Use these templates to achieve the designs shown in plates *30* and *31*.

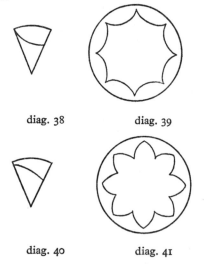

diag. 38   diag. 39

diag. 40   diag. 41

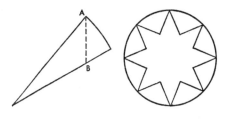

diag. 36   diag. 37

For a six-point pattern (diags. 42–45), fold the paper in half, and then into three. Fold in half again to make sure that both sides of the curve will be even. The paper circle must be folded from the middle each time, and each fold must be perfectly straight and even (pl. *80*).

Planning patterns for a square cake (pls. 32 and 35)

Cut a piece of paper the same size as the top of the cake. Fold in half, in half again, and then diagonally to form a triangle. Each fold must come from the centre. Draw two pencil lines as in diagram 46 from A to B, and from B to C. Cut through the pencil line.

To vary these patterns, cut the paper in diagram 38 deeper or shallower, and perhaps use the basically round pattern on a square cake or *vice versa*. Try several patterns before deciding which one to use: make more folds, or alternate the point and the curve (pl. *35*). Experiment by using one pattern inside another, perhaps placing the inner one off-centre (pl. *32*).

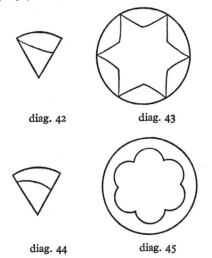

diag. 42   diag. 43

diag. 44   diag. 45

Making a template

Once each paper pattern is completed, place it on a sheet of thin cardboard with no folds or creases in it, and outline carefully. Using sharp scissors, cut out the design in cardboard. Make a small V-shaped cut in the centre so that the template can easily be lifted from the cake later. Keep the templates to be used several times over on different sized cakes.

How to use the template

This method is not practicable on a soft

icing like butter cream or glacé icing, as the surface would immediately be spoiled. It is excellent for use on cold fondant or hard royal icing as a basic guide to complete accuracy.

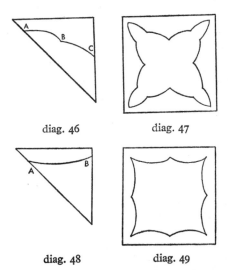

diag. 46   diag. 47

diag. 48   diag. 49

When the icing is quite firm and dry, and the surface is as perfect as possible, place the template in position, folding up the V-shape ready for lifting. Pipe round the template, one-eighth of an inch from the edge of the cardboard, using a number one or two icing tube. If the pattern is to be central, make sure that the points are all equi-distant from the edge before beginning to pipe. Break the line of icing at each point in the design, and join again neatly. It is not wise to try to work round a point.

Take great care to make good curves—lift the icing to work round a curve, lowering the line of icing into position. Only practice will achieve this to perfection.

When the design is completed, carefully lift off the template, using the raised cut of cardboard in the centre as a handle. On a white surface always pipe the first lines in white. If a mistake occurs, white lines can easily be removed with a knife, and re-piped correctly. Coloured lines may leave a mark if they are removed. To complete the design, over-pipe in white or colour.

Only the first line of piping round the template is needed before taking away the cardboard. Any further lines and decorations can be added freehand, parallel to the original design to give patterns inside one another. Emphasize the pattern by using tiny polka dots parallel to the first outline. Later, with more experience, pipe in lines of trellis, or groups of dots. But always, at first, practise the design on a practice board to achieve the correct balance and effect.

To make an eight-point star cake (pl. 29)

The specific cake in this photograph is a birthday cake. It has the eight-point star pattern worked in white royal icing, with a second line of pale-pink icing piped exactly on top. This outlining, or building-up makes a pattern stand out more. The centre is finished with three deeper-pink roses modelled from marzipan and arranged with maidenhair fern. The cake is circled with a pink ribbon to match the roses, the top edge and base of the cake neatened with a row of stars. This pattern is not difficult to execute—straight line patterns are always easier to achieve than curved designs. But one of the cardinal rules for success must always be remembered: never ice away, or "upwards". When necessary, turn the cake to achieve this.

Icing the cake board

On special-occasion cakes the silver board should be covered with a layer of white or coloured icing to match the cake. This should be done when the last coat is put on the cake. Spread a thin layer of icing on the board round the cake to the edge of the board. Put the cake on a turn-table and smooth the surface of the icing on the board with a palette knife, turning the cake at the same time. Clean the side edges of the board with a damp cloth before the icing has time to dry. When this smooth surface is quite set, decorate with trellis or braiding, and pipe dots, singly or in groups, round the edge of the board (pls. *30* to *32*).

A cake with trellis-work (pls. *30* and *31*)

This, as already explained, is fine parallel lines, crossing each other at right angles or diagonally. To fill an uneven space, begin with the centre line, and work parallel lines each side.

Braiding on a cake (pls. *32, 35* and *36*)

This simply signifies a fine line worked in and out continuously, like a jig-saw pattern. There should be no straight lines, no lines touching each other, and no breaks in the continuity. Braiding over a thin layer of smooth icing gives a dainty finish to the cake board or to the surrounds of an eight-point star design.

Decorating the sides of a royal iced cake

The most often used decoration on the side of a cake is the hanging piped loop. After practice, it is quite easily achieved freehand. Touch a point on the top edge of the cake and allow the icing to come from the tube in a loop. Let the loop hang in mid-air until it is the correct length, and then attach it further along the cake simply by touching the top edge again. At first there will be some failures and some breakages, but with practice on a tin or a practice model, these errors will soon be eliminated.

A beginner can, if necessary, cut a template for the loops, by cutting a strip of paper the circumference of the cake and folding it according to the size and number of the loops required. Draw a loop on the folded paper, or fold in half and draw half the loop. Cut through the pencil line, and open out. Hold in position round the cake with an elastic band. For complete accuracy with the freehand method, judge the position of the loops according to the pattern on the top surface of the cake, and mark the positioning with dots of icing. Study plates *31* and *35* to see the variety of ideas to be considered. Sometimes single loops are used, sometimes double loops. Most are elaborated with dots, either round or in between the loops.

But whatever pattern is attempted, it is always necessary to hold the tube away from the cake when making the loops, so that the icing falls into an even shape.

The closer to the cake the tube is held, the harder the task becomes.

An alternative method is to tilt the cake on a turntable and work the loops one-eighth of an inch from the curved loop template, as if making a pattern on the top of the cake. Remove the template and over-pipe the loops.

CHAPTER EIGHT

Baskets and Lettering in Royal Icing

Some of the most beautiful and the most elaborate cakes can be achieved through royal icing. A basket with sugar-pink roses is not difficult to make, the basket weaving tube is effective and does not require the practice that is needed for finer work. The only essential is patience, and an eye for perfection. The basket design is easy—in fact one of the easiest royal icing designs. This is why it appears early in the progress of this book.

MAKING A BASKET OF ROSES
(pls. *34, 37* and *38*)

Never attempt this with anything but a rich fruit cake, as much time may be needed to complete a basket, and the cake must last. The design is suitable for a birthday cake of any shape.

Cover the cake with almond paste and place on a silver cake board or drum two inches larger than the diameter of the cake. Coat with one layer of white or coloured royal icing. Do not trouble with a perfect finish, as the basket work will cover the surface. When the icing is dry, make basket work stakes using royal icing in a number four tube (pl. *33*), working from the base upwards to the top of the cake. Always make an even number of stakes on both round and square cakes. To be sure about this, count the stakes when they are nearly completed, and decide whether two or three should be fitted in to make up the even number. The stakes should be absolutely upright and parallel, about three-quarters of an inch apart all round the cake. Leave the stakes to dry.

Working a square or oblong lid (pls. *34* and *37*)

Use a thin silver board the size and shape of the cake surface to represent the basket lid. Make stakes three-quarters of an inch apart and parallel to each other straight onto the silver board. If the cake is oblong, cut the board in half and ice both halves with stakes to give the effect of a box lid opening at both sides from the centre.

The next day, when the stakes are dry, begin to form the weaving pattern. Using a fine ribbon tube number twenty-three, start at the bottom of the basket, holding the hand sideways so that the icing can be tucked under the icing stake. Bring it from one stake over the next stake, and tuck it under the third, breaking off cleanly. Repeat all round the base of the cake. Continue, alternating each row (diag. 50) until the whole of the side of the cake is covered in the weaving pattern. Weave square or oblong lids in the same way. Make a neat edge by piping a letter "*e*" with a number one or two tube continuously all round the base of the basket on the silver board, all round the top edge of the cake, and round the lid.

diag. 50

Working a round lid (pl. *38*)

Using a thin round silver board the same size as the top surface of the cake, make basket stakes as shown in diagram 51. Make the first stake across the centre of the board, and then cross it at right angles with the second. Divide into eighths with stakes reaching almost from the centre to the outer edge and continue halving each section until there is an even number of stakes three-quarters of an inch apart all the way round the edge of the basket lid.

diag. 51

Begin the weaving on the outside edge first, again working over alternate stakes so that the weaving appears to be continuous. Near the centre, it will be necessary to work over two or three stakes, but the end of every stake must be covered. Make the weaving as neat as possible, although it will almost always ⌐ as a square in the middle. Any mistakes that are made can usually be camouflaged with a bow of silk ribbon!

Filling the basket with roses

Make roses following the directions given in Chapter Four. Place the largest rose at the centre of one side of a square cake, or on the edge of a round cake. Using a knife or an icing bag cut to a number one tube, put a dab of icing on the rose, fixing in position with one of the curled back petals over the edge of the basket. Place the two largest of the remaining roses on each side of the first, and continue arranging according to size and colour until more than half the edge of the basket is covered. Place the lid in position, and adjust the roses so that the lid sits nicely in position. Arrange casually, pulling some roses out a little, pushing back others, and fitting in a few smaller roses where the board lid "hinges" on the cake at the back. Secure the lid in position with a little icing, making a continuous letter "*e*" to form a hinge.

The number of roses needed will vary according to the size of the cake and the size of the flowers. Generally, about twelve roses should be made for an eight-inch cake—any spare ones can always be saved for using in a later decoration. Any defects will be hidden, as before, by the ribbon bow across the top, which should tone in colour with the roses. A finishing touch can be given by inserting a sprig or two of pressed maidenhair fern or pressed asparagus fern between the roses.

A pleasant unexpected touch is added by writing a message of greeting on the cake before putting on the lid. This shows first as an extra surprise when the lid is removed, and the cake is about to be cut.

This basket work can also be made on a tin covered with waxed paper. Remove carefully and fill with sweets or even strawberries (pl. *50*).

LETTERING (pl. *36*)

Lettering, whether simple or elaborate, always adds to the pleasure given by an attractive, unusual cake. Simple script is naturally the easiest to achieve, but whatever writing is attempted, great care must be taken with accurate spacing. A perennial joke is made in the cartoons depicting a housewife icing "happy birt" on a cake because she has no space to finish the word. To ice a long word like *congratulations* or *anniversary* across the middle of a cake, it is advisable to write it first in pencil on a piece of paper the same size as the cake, or else to try out the lettering on the practice board.

If script is used, begin with the middle letter of the greeting, and work both ways to complete it accurately. It is never necessary to write across the centre of a cake—indeed, this is the least interesting arrangement. Place a motif in one corner, and write the greeting circling, or half-circling the motif—for accuracy, make a space guide with a piece of paper.

Fold a sheet of paper in half (diag. *52*) and cut a quarter-circle, or whatever shape is needed. Open out the paper (diag. 53) and use on the cake as a guide to positioning the letters. Write or print through the hole in the paper, and then remove the guide. For two words, e.g. *Christmas Greetings*, turn the paper upside down for the second word, as in diagram 54. This is effective, although even more unusual is the method of writing a word sideways (diag. 55). This shows to particularly good effect with a single spray of flowers.

Several types of lettering are suitable for icing. One of the most attractive is *Serif* lettering (diag. 56).

diag. 55

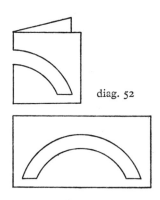

diag. 52

diag. 53

Practise by copying designs from magazines, greetings cards or newspapers, or books on Old English lettering. Stencils can also be bought and used as a guide for lettering, stiff icing put over them with a knife. When the stencil is removed, the work remains effectively and easily done. Always use firm icing for stencils, and not glacé icing (pl. *40*).

Vary style by using letters of uniform height, thickening the down stroke with a loop, designing a large first letter embellished with scroll work and tiny flowers (diag. 57), holding some of the smaller following letters (diag. 58). Fill in the outline of double letters with dots (diag. 56), or run-in with soft sugar. Turn to the back of the book for letters suitable for tracing and run-out work.

Experimentation is the keynote to good lettering. A greeting must be well done. Bad lettering can spoil an otherwise perfect cake.

diag. 54

diag. 56

diag. 57

diag. 58

CHAPTER NINE

Piping Sugar Flowers

To make icing flowers, keep practising on a practice board until perfect. This is the only way a good sugar flower can be achieved.

Most icing flowers are piped with a petal tube, numbers fifty-six to fifty-nine. The nozzle is shaped in a long slit, wide at one end, and very narrow at the other. Work on waxed paper, or on small squares of waxed paper on an icing nail or a cork top. Use very stiff royal icing, coloured delicately according to the flower.

SNOWDROPS (pl. 39)

These are the simplest flowers to pipe, as a single petal is sometimes sufficient for one flower, or two or three at the most for an open bloom. The effect relies on good positioning. A spray of snowdrops makes a dainty and appealing decoration placed in one corner of a cake.

diag. 59

Use the petal tube with the hollow side uppermost and the wider end down on the board. Use well-beaten white royal icing. Press out the icing, keeping the hand flat and moving round in a fanning movement. Each petal will resemble a tiny tooth. Pull off the tube with a quick downward movement. There will be a slight indentation in the centre of each petal, and a slightly raised curved edge (diag. 59).

To make a snowdrop with two petals, make one petal, and then pipe a second over-wrapping the first. For a snowdrop with three petals, make two petals beside each other but with a little space between them, and then place a third on top and in the centre. Work on a practice board until the art has been mastered, and then begin working on the waxed paper (pl. 39). After twenty-four hours, store the petals away in a box in a dry place, still on the waxed paper. When they are needed for use on a cake, pipe a small green bulb of icing and a hooked stem onto the cake, and place the sugar snowdrop in position with a little icing behind the flower to hold it in place. Using a litt¹ green colouring on an artist's paintbrush, make a few tiny green lines on the petals. Pipe green lines on the cake to represent leaves.

NARCISSI (pls. 40 and 41)

Again, work on a practice board at first, using white royal icing. Each flower has six petals placed adjoining each other in a circle (diag. 60). Touch the centre of the outer edge of each petal pulling out the icing, using the tube of icing or a pinhead to make a point as in the natural flower. Leave to dry, and then using a fine writer tube, make a spiral of icing to represent the trumpet. It is also possible, before adding the trumpet, to put one or three dots pulled up long in the centre of the flower, as the stamens and pistil.

When the complete flower is dry, paint the edge of the trumpet an orange colour, using edible colouring and a fine artist's brush.

sharply (diag. 62). When five petals have been completed allow to dry and then finish the centre with a tiny green dot, adding a few streaks of green and yellow edible colouring from the centre with

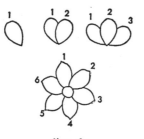

diag. 60

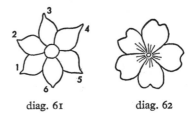

diag. 61   diag. 62

an artist's brush. If possible, look at a natural flower or a good picture before adding these final details.

DAISY-TYPE FLOWERS

Use almost any colour icing: white for a field daisy or marguerite; mauve for a Michaelmas daisy; orange for marigolds; pink for pyrethrum, etc. Holding the petal tube at right angles to the waxed paper, with the wide part to the centre of the flower, press only very gently, and pull off the tube quickly. Make any number of petals, placing them closely in a circle, with no hole in the centre. For a daisy with wider petals, turn the tube the opposite way.

With practice, almost any flower can be represented, even a chrysanthemum. Use ingenuity and imagination, as there is not enough space here to describe every type of flower in such an enormous range.

DAFFODILS (pls. *40* and *41*)

Using yellow icing, follow the directions given for making narcissi. As each petal is made, touch the centre carefully, drawing it out in a longer point. A cocktail stick may be easier to use than the icing tube. Work the petals from left to right (diag. 61), taking great care when icing the last petal not to spoil the first. Raise the tube a little to complete the last petal.

When the petals are dry, centre them with a long pistil, and make a yellow trumpet slightly deeper than for a narcissus. Finish the last time round with a wavy line to give the effect of a crimped edge. Vary the shade of the trumpet colour to deeper or paler yellow, or even to white. There are so many varieties of daffodils that it is almost impossible to go wrong with the shading.

PANSIES (pls. *39* and *43*)

Although these are difficult, wonderful effects can be achieved with patience. Practise on the board before attempting the flowers on waxed paper, and follow closely the order for icing each petal, given in diagram 63. Icing can always be scraped off a board back into the basin to be used

PRIMROSES

Make five petals for each flower from a pale greeny-yellow icing. Move the hand up and down to form a heart shape, almost as if making two petals, and pull off again, but never scrape off waxed paper, as grease may spoil the icing in the bowl.

Use two different colours for making a pansy, e.g., colour the two top petals yellow, and the rest mauve, or *vice versa*. Make petal 1 first, with 2 slightly over it. Then 3 and 4, and finally number 5, which is usually twice the size of the others. When making this last petal the first four petals should be upside down.

When the flower is quite dry, paint in the face with edible colour and a fine brush. Finish the centre with a dot of yellow. Again, look at a natural flower or picture to help perfect the colouring—two colours at once in the tube can give an unusual effect.

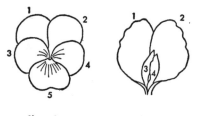

diag. 63   diag. 64

VIOLETS (pls. *11* and *41*)

Make these like pansies, using mauve or purple icing. This is a hard colour to obtain, and sometimes, instead of the real deep dark-violet colour, pale wild violets have to be substituted. Centre with a green dot pulled out long with a tiny red dot on the end.

SWEET PEAS (pl. *39*)

Using pink, white or mauve icing in varying shades, make two petals together with a slight frill at the edges. Make two smaller, fatter petals together, holding the tube at right angles to the first petals, and raising it in an upwards and downwards movement (diag. 64). Pull off quickly. This flower needs a lot of practice—it is difficult to describe, but with patience a student can soon teach herself. With sweet peas, as with pansies, two colours in a tube are very effective.

Forget-me-nots, dog roses, etc., can all be made with sugar icing, following these basic directions. Five dots close together in a circle will form these small coloured flowers, with a centre dot of yellow. Larger flowers can be worked in blue or pink icing following the directions for a narcissus, but simply inserting a yellow dot in the flower centre.

SUGAR-CENTRED FLOWERS

Rub two or three drops of green, yellow or brown edible colouring into a little castor or granulated sugar. Pipe some varying sized bulbs of icing on waxed paper, and before the icing is dry, sprinkle with the coloured sugar. Touch gently with the finger to make the sugar stick to the icing. Shake off any surplus sugar and leave to dry. Make daisy-type flowers, and while still wet, place one of these coloured centres in position, using the most suitable size to the flower. Perhaps make a double row of petals, piping the outer row first, with a space in the middle. Allow to dry, and then add a second row on top. Add the sugar centre to give the effect of a dahlia or sunflower.

In place of sugar it is possible to use *non-pareils*, more generally known as Hundreds and Thousands.

Use these sugar-coated bulbs of icing to represent mimosa and willow catkins on an Easter cake (pl. *42*), or to make small chickens or ducklings, coating the wet icing with yellow castor sugar to give a soft downy effect. Use brown shades of sugar to give more effect to small decorations depicting dogs, cats and birds.

TEA ROSES (pl. *87*)

Pipe the flowers onto the end of a cocktail stick, working from left to right with the thin end of the tube uppermost. Make the first petal over the top of the stick; the second over-lapping one-third of the first; and the third over-lapping one-third again, so that the three petals form a circle. Continue making petals round the stick until the rose is the right size. Have ready some waxed paper, and pushing the pointed end of the cocktail stick through the paper, draw it through until the rose is left on the paper. This method ensures that the petals are held up.

Pipe tiny rosebuds onto a pin-head and stick the pin in a pincushion until the icing is dry. Make larger flowers on a skewer, removing by cutting the edge of the waxed paper, placing the skewer in the slit, and drawing it downwards, leaving behind the flower.

These flowers, too, are most effective piped with two shades of icing in the tube at once.

LEAVES

Green leaves to accompany the flowers can be made with a leaf tube, although generally this is only suitable for larger flowers. A paper bag only gives better results for piping small leaves.

Fill the greaseproof paper bag as usual, pressing the end flat between the thumb and finger. Cut the point in an inverted letter V like an arrow-head—for small leaves, cut only one-eighth of an inch from each side. Begin to pipe with the paper bag touching the waxed paper, and the end turning upwards. Press gently, and as the icing begins to come from each side of the V, slightly raise the bag, press out to the correct size, and pull off quickly to form a point at the end of the leaf. Alternatively make long, thin leaves to accompany daffodils, or a serrated fern-like leaf by moving the tube carefully backwards and forwards.

The best method of making a specific type of leaf is soon found by experimenting on the practice board. Make on waxed paper to be stored away for future use, or when proficient, pipe straight onto the cake (pl. *33*).

White royal icing leaves can also be made—generally used for neatening and decorating wedding cakes. To give the effect of a vein to these leaves make a tiny cut in the centre of the V in the piping bag. For larger leaves cut a larger V shape, re-shaping the V cut with sharp scissors as the bag becomes worn. Re-press the end of the bag frequently between the thumb and finger.

WATER LILIES (pl. *126*)

These are also made with the bag only, cut as for leaves in the shape of a letter V. Practise first on the board, and when proficient, pipe the flowers straight onto waxed paper. Make three or four petals in a circle, pulling upwards into long points instead of pulling out into a leaf shape. Touch the petal carefully, coaxing it to stand up, and even to curl inwards a little. Continue making petals outside the first three or four, until there are about eighteen in all, piped close together. Finally add a few yellow dots in the centre and small green run-out leaves described in Chapter Fourteen.

APPLE BLOSSOM (pl. *101*)

Fill a petal tube with pink icing in the thin side, and white in the thick side. Before beginning to ice, press out into the bowl of pink icing until both pink and white are coming from the tube. Begin piping with the tube on its side, the hollow side towards the worker, the thick end on the board and the thin end in the air. Press out a curled petal, and putting the tube inside the first petal, press out a second. Make five petals in all, to form a cup-shaped flower.

Although a small petal tube will make hawthorn, cherry and peach blossom, the bigger tube is more effective for apple blossom. Finish with a few long yellow dots in the flower centre. Arrange the blossoms on a twig by making a roll of marzipan coloured brown and broken into differing lengths. A few green leaves iced straight onto the branch with the blossom are very effective.

If a petal tube is not available, it is possible to make flowers using a paper bag only. Cut as for leaves, and make a series of petals working from the centre, pulling the bag out to the sides or edges of each petal. To finish, pipe the flower centre using a bag cut with a small round hole.

Using this method, the petals will be more pointed than those made with the correct petal tube, but for some flowers this is quite an advantage, and with practice, quite a degree of success can be achieved.

CHAPTER TEN

Easter Novelties and Chocolate Work

There is much more pleasure in making—and in giving—an Easter egg made and decorated at home, than in giving a silver-wrapped chocolate egg seen in dozens of shops all over the country. And the variety, instead of limited to the range in the local shops, is endless and fascinating. Some Easter novelties are easy to make. Some are more difficult. But with practice, and with patience, even the beginner can learn to make them all.

DECORATED ALMONDS

These are useful as Easter novelties, as they can be used to represent eggs. Buy some good quality sugared almonds in various colours. Using a paper icing bag only, fill with coloured royal icing and cut a very small hole. Make line and dot flowers—daisies, dandelions, marguerites, Michaelmas daisies and even daffodils and hyacinths composed of dots, adding green stems and leaves (diag. 65). When more proficient, short names can be piped onto the almonds.

separately in small paper cases and arrange in a cellophane box.

DECORATED EASTER EGGS
(pls. *44* and *48*)

If Easter egg moulds are available, it is possible to make eggs with chocolate—described later in this chapter—otherwise, buy some plain chocolate Easter eggs. Have ready a quantity of piped sugar flowers (for making, see instructions in previous chapter). Try out arrangements of flowers on the practice board first to perfect balance and colour and to ensure adequate space is left to pipe the child's name.

Scratch the surface of the chocolate egg with a sharp, pointed tool—e.g. a long needle—put on a dot of icing, and fix the flower before the icing has time to dry. When the arrangement is complete, pipe in green stems. An icing bow can be made, using the serrated ribbon tube. If a large egg is being decorated, make the bow on waxed paper and leave to dry before putting in place. Small marzipan roses are

diag. 65

This is good practice in the careful, fine work needed for more advanced designs, and with a little care and patience, delightful effects can be achieved.

When completed, place the almonds

also suitable for decorating Easter eggs, cutting off some of the base of the roses as soon as they are made, so that they are not too long to place on the egg.

Neaten the join of the egg with a row of

icing shells or scrolls, or tie round with a piece of ribbon, silver braid or lace. The final effect should be one of prettiness and daintiness.

Place the finished egg in the centre of a square of cellophane. Draw up to the top and fasten with an elastic band. If the egg has no ribbon, tie the cellophane with a ribbon bow. The whole effect is expensive and professional, and at the same time the egg is hygienically covered.

RABBITS
MADE FROM EASTER EGGS

Use a small egg for the rabbit head, and a larger one for the body. Pipe the face on the tiny egg, complete with ears and whiskers. White dots of royal icing with chocolate centres make the eyes. Use icing to fix the small egg in a suitable position on the larger egg, and pipe icing lines or use rolls of marzipan for front and back legs. Place in a box on a bed of green paper straw, or arrange on green shredded coconut.

HENS AND CHICKENS
MADE FROM EASTER EGGS

Using red or yellow gum paste or pastillage (*see* Chapter Thirteen), roll out thinly, and cut out a red cock's comb or a small yellow crest, and place in position on the egg, fixing with royal icing. Make the beak in the same way, and pipe in the eyes. Cover with cellophane as described previously, and put in a box.

NATURAL HENS' EGGS
FOR EASTER

Before boiling the egg for breakfast, draw a face on the shell using a blue wax crayon for the eyes, black for eyebrows and lashes, and adding a red heart-shaped mouth and brown hair. Make a simple paper hat or bonnet using a little glue and bright coloured crêpe paper. Boil the eggs as usual for Easter morning breakfast, place in the egg-cups, put on the hats and bonnets, and the result is an amusing novelty for the start of Easter.

AN EASTER EGG CRADLE

Using two halves of a hollow Easter egg, place the smaller end of one half into the larger end of the other half, tilting slightly to form a cradle with a canopy. Fasten in position with royal icing. Roll out white marzipan or cold fondant icing to form a coverlet, make a cradle pillow, and mould a small figure for the baby. Assemble the whole cradle, and finally pipe lines of trellis and lace work on the coverlet (pl. *43*).

CHOCOLATE WORK

Always carry out chocolate work in a medium temperature. Too hot a temperature prevents chocolate from setting, and too cold a temperature will make it set too quickly and may also cause it to set dull instead of shiny.

Tempering chocolate

For large-scale production of chocolate work it is necessary to "temper" the chocolate.

Break up the plain chocolate and melt in a double saucepan with water in the outer pan hot but not boiling. Melt the chocolate to 100°–115°F. Stir well, remove the pan of chocolate to a pan of cold water and cool to 80°–82°F., stirring thoroughly. Replace the pan of chocolate on the hot water and re-heat to 88°–90°F., stirring all the time. The chocolate is now ready for use. For best results use a thermometer.

For milk chocolate use 2°F. lower temperature in each case.

For cake coating use a good brand of covering chocolate broken into small pieces and put into a double saucepan or a basin covered with a saucer. Allow some water to come to the boil and place the double pan or covered basin in position on

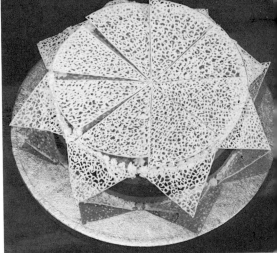

65. *Above*—A pale green cold fondant surface covered with white lace triangles each with one side slightly lifted to give a 'windmill' effect.

64. *Above*—Dainty white Christmas cake decorated with letters run-out in lace triangles and a circle of red ribbon and holly.

66. *Right*—Pink sugar lace triangles decorate a cake iced in deeper pink cold fondant.

67. *Left*—A ballet dancer lace triangle cake iced in lavender and pink.

68. Lace collar cake decorated with poinsettias.

69. Birthday cake of forget-me-nots and pale blue lace work.

70. *Left*—Christening cake—to make the stork use wire bent to form head and neck and rolled round finger to form body, tapering towards tail and fixed to two wire legs; cover with icing and when dry ice in the wing shape; make legs long to push into the cake and ice feet straight on to cake surface.

71. *Right*—Figures '25' worked in trellis on a silver wedding cake.

72. *Left*—Lace work cake for a ballet enthusiast.

73. *Centre*—Christmas cake using a plaque of the nativity scene surrounded by lace shells made on a teaspoon, four cushions and braiding on the board.

74. *Bottom left*—Cake using cushions and butterflies.

75. *Bottom right*—Cake using eight cushions.

76. *Left*—Square cake using two types of raised lace work: the cushions and a dome made over an egg poacher; pastillage flowers finish the design.

77. *Centre left*—A dainty fan-edged birthday cake centred with a lace 'plate' holding pink roses and maidenhair fern.

78. *Centre right*—A square fan-edged cake with orange roses on a lacework 'plate'.

79. *Left*—Raised lines of piping shield fronds of maidenhair fern on a simple white Christmas cake.

80. *Right*—Simple cake finished with scroll edging and decorated with a six point star, piped narcissi and raised baskets holding fern.

81. *Left*—Springtime birthday cake using piped spring flowers and raised lace work sections.

82. *Right*—Birthday cake decorated with a raised lace vase filled with piped red roses.

83. *Left*—Dainty lace work flower decoration worked on bent tin and edged with scrolls and dots.

84. *Left*—A clock face design decorated with raised lace and braiding.

85. *Right*—Raised lace work and orange blossom flowers finish a horse-shoe shaped silver wedding cake.

86. *Bottom left*—A 'happy birthday' cake decorated with red roses and a lace fan.

87. *Bottom right.* Raised lace and run-out work make a colourful scenic cake, although the photograph does not do justice to the intricate miniature wrought iron gate of raised icing.

89. *Below*—A boat-shaped piece of lace icing, placed upside down, holds a decoration of tiny run-out flowers and a lace butterfly.

88. *Above*—Engagement cake decorated with a spray of spring flowers and heart-shaped lace work.

90. *Below*—Neat scrolls edge a birthday cake centred with a piped lace icing 'doily'. Run-out blossom petals are used on the board to make flowers.

91. *Above*—A raised platform of gum paste holds water-lilies surrounded by braiding and raised lace work. Fish decorate the cake sides.

92. *Top left*—Raised lace work and a spray of piped violets make a good angled design for a square cake.

93. *Top right*—Tragacanth baskets and handles in varying shapes and sizes.

94. *Centre left*—A boy's horseshoe 21st birthday cake with old English lettering, neat scroll edging and raised lace 'nails'.

95. *Bottom left*—Two 'pages' of a pastillage Christmas card, ready to be tied together with ribbon and a second card decorated with a thin circular pastillage plaque.

the almost boiling water. Do not allow the water to boil or the chocolate will become lumpy. Remove immediately from the heat and leave to stand for a while. When the water is cool, the chocolate will be ready.

When the chocolate has had time to melt, remove from the water and beat with a wooden spoon without letting any water or steam get into the chocolate. Have the cake ready on a plate with a doyley, and pour the chocolate onto the centre of the cake, coaxing it over the top surface just to the edge, in the same way as a glacé icing. Leave undisturbed to set. When set, pipe with a simple pattern as described later in this chapter.

CHOCOLATE BOXES (pl. 45)

While the chocolate is melting, lay on a flat surface a piece of waxed paper from a breakfast cereal packet or a sliced loaf wrapping. When the chocolate is melted, beat and pour onto the waxed paper. Spread evenly with a knife, and make a neat, straight edge. Leave to set a little, and as soon as the chocolate is beginning to darken, cut into two-inch squares with a knife. Leave to become quite hard.

Meanwhile, prepare pink butter cream, squares of Madeira or Genoese sponge cake, slightly smaller than the chocolate squares. Using the cream or some jam, fix four squares of chocolate, one to each side of the cake squares, using as the outside, the chocolate that was next to the waxed paper. Pipe a large butter cream rosette in the top and arrange a lid of chocolate at an angle, as in plate 45.

CHOCOLATE TORTON

Melt the chocolate as before—about a quarter of a pound of chocolate to cover a seven-inch cake—a further two ounces for the sides. Meanwhile, cut a circle of waxed paper the size of the outside of the bottom of the tin in which the cake—a chocolate mixture or a Madeira—has been baked.

Also cut a strip of waxed paper the right size to go round the cake, with a little extra length in case of breakages. When the chocolate is ready, pour onto both pieces of waxed paper, coaxing it over to the edge of the circle, and spreading it the length of the strip.

When the chocolate begins to darken, cut through the centre of the circle, and diagonally in eight or twelve positions to make triangles according to the size of the pieces of cake required. Cut the strip into pieces half an inch wide. Leave to set. Meanwhile, make about four or six ounces of butter cream, coloured and flavoured with cocoa or instant coffee. Spread the cake top evenly, and if necessary put in a filling.

Spread jam or cream round the side of the cake, and carefully lifting the half-inch strips arrange them round the cake, in each case using the side that has been next to the waxed paper as the outside. Pipe eight or twelve stars on top of the cake at even places—pipe these rather tall to raise the chocolate triangles. Set the triangles at a slant on the stars, again with the smooth side uppermost, and with the points to the centre, like an electric fan. Finally, pipe a scroll of butter cream on each triangle and a rosette in the centre of the cake (pl. 46). Before serving, tie a piece of gilt cord in a bow round the cake to hold the chocolate strips in place. If preferred, chocolate vermicelli can be used on the side of the cake instead of the chocolate strips.

For a games party, make the cake shown in plate 47. Follow the method just described for making the chocolate shapes, using metal cutters or templates for the hearts, diamonds, spades and clubs designs.

PIPING CHOCOLATE

Draw the shapes required—wheels, snow-flakes, hearts, etc.—on greaseproof paper, and then cover with thin waxed paper. Melt the chocolate and beat well, adding at the most two or three drops of glycerine to a quarter of a pound of chocolate. Beat again, cool a little, and put into a greaseproof paper piping bag as for royal icing. Pipe onto the waxed paper, following the sketches on the greaseproof paper underneath. As well as simple shapes, pipe scrolls in batches (pl. *56*), chocolate hearts (pl. *55*); a music clef and notes; swans' heads to top cream bodies on a fruit gateau (pl. *49*). When set, remove these shapes from the waxed paper and store until required. A simple design need not always be made beforehand, but can be piped straight onto the chocolate-coated cake.

CHOCOLATE EASTER EGGS
(pls. *44* and *48*)

Special moulds must be bought to make chocolate eggs. When not in use, always keep in a paper bag in an airtight tin to protect from the atmosphere, and before using, polish up the inside of the mould by rubbing with a piece of cotton wadding. If necessary for easy removal of the chocolate egg shape, grease the moulds slightly with castor oil, rubbing well to remove any surplus. Avoid making fingermarks on the inside of the mould as these would show on the chocolate egg.

Pour the melted chocolate into the egg mould and run it round to cover the entire inside surface to the edges. Pour out the surplus chocolate before it can begin to set. Put into a cold place immediately. Never put into a refrigerator, as the intense cold would shrink the chocolate too quickly. When the chocolate is set it will have shrunk slightly. Pare the edge with a palette knife, and using the same knife, remove the chocolate carefully from the mould—sometimes it can be shaken out. Take care not to break the egg shape.

To fix together the two halves of an egg, heat water to almost boiling point in an aluminium saucepan, and carefully and quickly brush the edge of the egg across the outside of the warm pan. Just as

quickly, put the two egg halves together. The melted chocolate should seal to make a complete egg. This needs practice, but it is a very practical way of doing the job.

If moulds are available, animals can also be made in this way.

CHOCOLATE CUPS AND BASKETS

Cover the inside surface of tinfoil baking cups with melted chocolate, following the directions given for making chocolate eggs, pouring out the surplus chocolate. Alternatively, use double greaseproof paper cases. Cool very quickly. Remove when quite cold, peeling the paper away. Fill the chocolate "bowl" with a truffle mixture of cake crumbs, butter cream, and jam, adding chopped cherries, nuts and a flavouring of rum or vanilla. Spread the top evenly, cover with glacé icing, and decorate with a star of butter cream and a handle of bent angelica or chocolate which has previously been piped into an arch shape on waxed paper.

Put the handle on the side to make a chocolate cup, or over the top, for a chocolate basket.

HOME-MADE CHOCOLATES

Chocolate centres can be made from marzipan cut into shapes, very stiff royal icing rolled into balls, or pieces of crystalized fruits. Lower one centre at a time into melted chocolate using a dipping fork. Remove and shake off the surplus chocolate drawing it across the side of the pan. Place the chocolate on waxed paper or rack to set. Arrange in individual papers in a fancy box.

It is necessary to temper the chocolate first if any quantity is required or if they are to be kept any length of time. If tempering is omitted the chocolate sets slowly and may be without gloss and have a patchy appearance.

CHAPTER ELEVEN

Party Biscuits and Cakes

As a change from the intense concentration needed to ice an elaborate cake, ice novelty biscuits for a children's party or a Valentine's Day tea. Let the imagination run riot and design beautiful old-fashioned ladies in crinoline skirts or chocolate sponge engines and pop-eyed gingerbread men to delight the children.

FEATHER ICING BISCUITS (pl. 52)

Use plain bought tea biscuits or make Shrewsbury biscuits (recipe at back of book). Cut into rounds about three or four inches across. When baked and cold, ice with white or pale-coloured glacé icing. Have ready an icing bag of glacé icing flavoured and coloured with cocoa or edible colouring. While the glacé icing is still wet, pipe straight lines half an inch apart across the biscuit, and while both surface and piping are still wet, draw a knife at right angles through the piping lines, again at intervals of half an inch (diag. 66), producing a loop effect.

Ice and pipe exactly the same design on a second biscuit, but draw the knife across in lines one inch apart, turn the biscuit round, and draw the knife back in lines again one inch apart, between the previous cuts, making a feather pattern, similar to the cake in plate 26.

On another biscuit, pipe circles, beginning with a small circle in the centre, and encircling it with larger circles, each one half an inch outside the other. Draw a knife from the centre outwards in eight positions, as if cutting a cake. This produces a spider's web effect (diag. 67). Alternatively, draw the knife from the outside to the middle in the same eight positions, or draw the knife outwards in

quarters, and divide each quarter by drawing the knife inwards, or *vice versa*. These two patterns produce an attractive flower design.

As another, completely different design, pipe diametrical lines dividing the biscuit into eight parts, and draw the knife round and round in a circular movement (diag. 68). This gives a pinwheel effect.

Vary the icing colours and try out different patterns. Always eat these biscuits the same day they are iced while they are crisp. The same patterns may be used on cakes.

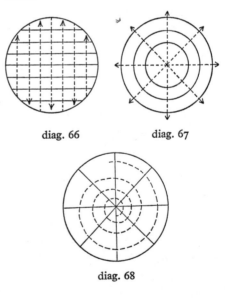

diag. 66   diag. 67

diag. 68

"LADIES' FINGERS"

Buy a packet of sponge finger biscuits or make sponge finger cakes. Using royal icing in a number one tube, pipe a line round the edge of the biscuit. Make glacé icing, and cover the surface of the biscuit inside the piped area. Bring the glacé icing just to the line but do not break or the icing will flow over the edge.

When set, using the icing bag only, pipe a wavy trail of green royal icing the length of each biscuit to represent a stem. When every line is completed, cut the bag pointed to make tiny leaves shooting at intervals from the green trail. At the top of each trail add a circle of white or bright-coloured dots in royal icing, centred with a yellow dot, to form a flower. Alternatively, at intervals on the stem add any red marzipan berries left over from making holly.

VALENTINE BISCUITS
(pls. 13 and 53)

Roll out a Shrewsbury biscuit mixture to about one-eighth of an inch in thickness. Cut into heart shapes with a cutter or by folding a piece of paper in half, drawing on it half of a heart shape, cutting through the pencil line, and opening out a heart-shaped paper guide (diag. 69). Lay this on the biscuit pastry and cut round with a knife.

diag. 69

Place the shapes on a greased baking-tray and cook at No. 3 or 4 regulo until pale-brown—avoid overbaking and turn round frequently to bake evenly. When pale-brown transfer to a wire tray, using a fish slice if necessary. The biscuits will become firm when cold. Make one or two special Valentines, about six inches across, giving plenty of scope for piping elaborate designs.

The ways of decorating Valentine biscuits are endless—sprays of piped flowers and raised lace patterns are just two ideas out of many. When the biscuits are cool, ice a line about a quarter of an inch all round the edge of the biscuit, using white royal icing and a number one tube. Fill the centre with white or pale-coloured glacé icing, or royal icing thinned out with a little water or white of egg. On the outside of the piped line, when the centre is dry, pipe a lace edge to the biscuit, consisting of dots: two dots together, topped with a third dot on the outside, at intervals round the edge, or pyramids of dots, starting with three, then two, and then one (pl. 53). Alternate different ideas of lacy points, scallops and fringes, and complete with flower arrangements and letters. See Chapter Twelve for more advanced, intricate lace work designs.

ANIMAL BISCUITS

Again using a Shrewsbury biscuit recipe, cut out animal or figure shapes with cutters, or make a paper pattern and cut out with a knife, as the heart-shape biscuits were made. Suitable animal shapes can often be cut from newspaper advertisements or tracings taken from children's picture books. Pipe round the edge of the figure and fill the centre with glacé or thinned royal icing. When dry, pipe in the face, and outline any clothing.

GINGERBREAD MEN

These are quick and easy to make, as very little detail is required. Use a ginger biscuit or ginger pastry recipe. Roll a ball for the head about the size of a thimble, and another about the size of an egg for the body. Make two rolls for the legs and two for the arms. Flatten out in position on a greased baking sheet, placing the head, arms and legs against the body. Leave plenty of room between the figures, as the mixture will spread. Bake, and remove carefully with a fish slice. When partly cooled, transfer to a wire tray. When quite cold, pipe the face, and perhaps add a hat and buttons.

Gingerbread donkeys can be made using the same method.

GINGERBREAD HOUSE

Make a pattern for a square house, or cut up a suitable size cardboard box and use in the same way. Use four pieces for walls, two for the roof, and perhaps two further pieces to represent a fence and a gate. Grease the back of the cardboard, lay it on the rolled-out pastry, and cut to shape. Bake all the pieces flat, use a fish slice to remove from the baking-sheet, and cool on a wire tray.

When quite cold, fix the house together, using royal icing on the inside to join the pieces. Prop with jars until the icing is quite firm, and then pipe in royal icing doors and windows. Stand the house on a silver board covered with green coconut or rough green icing, to represent grass. Add the fence and gate and a few piped flowers. Chocolate drops can be used to tile the roof, and a gingerbread man put in the garden. There is no end to the scope, and the fun to be had making this novelty.

BISCUIT CLOCKS

Bake round Shrewsbury biscuits, pipe a circle round the edge, and cover the centre with glacé icing. When dry, pipe on the numbers and the clock hands. These can be iced straight onto the biscuit surface, but the piping does not always stick well.

"FUNNY-FACE" BISCUITS

Pipe eyes, nose and mouth in coloured icing onto round pink-iced Shrewsbury biscuits. The funnier the faces, the more amusing the result, and the more popular the biscuits will be with children.

* * *

Children's stencil painting packets are often useful for quick letter and picture decorations on a cake. Use a surface of royal icing or cold fondant, as the stiff parchment paper could spoil a soft surface of glacé icing.

Find a suitable pattern, place the stencil in position on the cake, and spread quickly with a stiff royal or fudge icing. Remove the stencil carefully, leaving behind the pattern. Add any necessary outlining or details in royal icing.

CHILDREN'S PARTY CAKES

Large letter or number stencils can be used to good effect on small, square cakes to represent building bricks, chocolate swiss rolls modelled into an engine (pl. 54) and spelling bricks at a party for tiny children.

Cover square pieces of cake with different coloured cold fondant icings. With the finger, rub cornflour gently across the surface for a smooth finish. Using large stencil letters and numbers, spread royal icing across, allowing one side to dry before making a second letter on another side. Alternatively, the numbers can be piped onto the cakes.

For variety, stencil bold simple scenes: ducks or chickens following each other, houses, or a figure with balloons.

Bought plain biscuits, or home-made ones, iced with run-out royal icing (see Chapter Fourteen), can be stencilled easily, and make pretty place names for a children's party. For savouries, stencil cream cheese onto plain biscuits, making a name, a picture, or any simple design.

A variation on these methods is to dredge icing sugar over a stencil. Dredge the word LEMON across a lemon cake, ORANGE on an orange cake, and so on, or place a doyley on a cake and dredge over with icing sugar for a quick sponge decoration. Remove the doyley, leaving behind the sugar pattern.

* * *

Butter cream is an excellent medium for piping quick designs. It is a soft icing, it can be flavoured, and it takes colour well. Follow the recipe given in Chapter One, but only begin piping with butter cream when well practised with royal icing. Make a slightly larger greaseproof bag, using paper about eight or nine inches by twelve inches, and cut across diagonally, as in the making of royal icing bags. Cut off the end of the bag, and insert a number five or eight star tube, according to the work.

ICING A BAR CAKE

Use an oblong Madeira or light fruit cake, baked in a loaf tin. Coat the sides with jam or butter cream and chopped nuts or toasted coconut. Using the star tube and a natural-coloured butter cream, pipe a line down each of the long edges on the top of the cake, and a line down the centre. Colour the remaining butter cream pink, and again using the star tube, work a line of close zig-zagging between the two lines of natural-coloured cream. This should cover the entire top surface of the cake. Finally, add a little cocoa to the pink cream and pipe stars half an inch apart along the top of the central line. Make these stars by holding the star tube near the work and pressing out the icing until the star is the right size. Stop pressing and pull off quickly but carefully. Try this out first on a practice board.

CHOCOLATE HEARTS CAKE (pl. 55)

Coat the sides of a sponge or Genoese sandwich cake with cream and chopped nuts. Fill a paper icing bag with red or green piping jelly (this can be bought, but if unobtainable, use sieved apricot jam, either natural-coloured, or with red or green edible colouring added). Pipe lines of jelly across the cake diagonally, dividing the surface into eight parts. Using the star tube, pipe natural colour cream zig-zags into each section, beginning in the centre and working to the outside, making the lines gradually longer to cover the

whole of each section. To give variety, colour may be used in alternate sections. Decorate the top with piped chocolate hearts (see Chapter Ten), cherries or piped flowers.

USING THE SCRAPER PATTERN

Attempt this only on the firmer cakes—Madeira or a Victoria sandwich. Spread the top and sides with hot apricot glaze, and when set and cold, cover the surface as smoothly as possible with a thin layer of butter cream. Leave to set in a refrigerator or any cold place. When set, spread more thickly with cream, and use the scraper pattern shown in plate 56. Pipe zigzag lines from the centre of the cake in pale-pink, green or orange cream and finish each end with a large star. Have ready some piped chocolate shapes and arrange round the edge of the cake, adding piped flowers to tone with the colour of the cream. Neaten the lower edge, as well as the top edge, with a scroll, shell or star, practising the scrolls on the board first, holding the tube in the same way as for a star, and moving it round into the sideways question mark line. Pull off quickly so that the scroll thins out to nothing, and fit the second scroll on the trail of the first. A shell is made as if making a star, but bring the tube forward and straight down, pulling off quickly, pressing out only the necessary amount of icing for the shell (pls. 33 and 82).

MAKING A CRINOLINE LADY (pl. 57)

This is a quick decoration that looks very attractive and intricate. Bake a Madeira cake mixture in a "Pyrex" or oven glass basin, using about half a pound of flour to a one and a half pint basin. Grease the basin well and put two strips of paper in the base and up the sides. Bake the mixture for about an hour to an hour and a quarter, as the basin is thick, and the cake deep. Remove the cake from the basin with the paper strips and cool thoroughly. Cut the top level, coat the sides with apricot glaze if necessary, and place upside down on a silver board. Have ready a china model head.

Make up butter cream using four ounces of margarine with four ounces of sifted icing sugar. Beat well. Spread the front of the cake smoothly to represent the apron front, and mark in pleats with a knife. Avoid pulling up crumbs from the cake—this does not happen if apricot glaze has been used. With a star tube, and a paper icing bag rather larger than usual as a lot of cream will be needed, make four loops of natural-coloured butter cream to join each side of the apron,

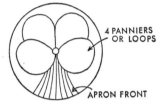

4 PANNIERS OR LOOPS

APRON FRONT

diag. 70

representing panniers (diag. 70). Fill in the loops with natural colour stars, fitted in close together. Keeping back enough natural-coloured cream for bows and decoration, colour the remainder to match the china head. Using the coloured cream, pipe stars close together covering the entire remainder of the cake right down to the board.

To finish, add colour to the cream put aside, and using a number one tube, pipe decorations of dots and hanging loops on the apron front, and add three bows at the top of the loops or panniers. Place the china doll's head in position and neaten the waistline with some cream. Leave in a cool place to set.

This basic design can be varied in several ways, perhaps by including frills, piped with a petal tube.

* * *

For special occasions, savoury piping can be both useful, and attractive. All the early preparations can be done beforehand, and the actual assembling of each novelty takes very little time.

COCKTAIL SAVOURIES

Use plain biscuits, cheese-flavoured biscuits, home-made pastry cut into shapes, toast or fried bread. Never add the piping too long before the snacks are to be eaten, as the crisp biscuits will become soft and disappointing. Have ready a selection of foods to be used: a soft cream cheese that can be piped, butter, radishes, peas, cucumber, ham, tinned salmon, potted meat, walnuts and pickled walnuts, hard-boiled eggs, carefully mashed potatoes, tomato paste, parsley and cress.

If there are a lot of savouries to make, add a little white sauce and mashed potato to help eke out the cheese, and for a different flavour and colour add some tomato paste and seasoning to a little of the cheese mixture. Colour a little of the butter with green colouring, and a little with red. Have all these mixtures prepared first, and then spread the biscuits with butter and cover some of them with ham, cooked meat, cucumber or any other suitable surface, cut to shape.

Using a star tube, pipe lines or stars of white cream cheese on all the biscuits. Changing to the cheese and tomato paste, add more lines and stars, or make varied daisy or straight line patterns. Decorate the tops with tiny pieces of pickled walnut, gherkin or carrot, etc.

Meanwhile, dissolve two teaspoons of aspic jelly or gelatine in one-eighth pint warm water, and leave until on the point of setting. Have the savouries ready on a wire tray, and coat thinly with the setting jelly.

When set, transfer to dainty trays or plates and garnish with cress, finishing with fine lines of the coloured butter, piped in a whirl or zigzag over the top of the biscuits with a number one plain tube or a paper bag only. There is no end to the ideas that can be used to decorate these savouries (pl. 15).

CHAPTER TWELVE

Raised Lace Work

This is perhaps the most delicate of all icing work, and yet when it is expertly carried out, it is remarkable how easily the pieces can be handled without breaking.

As a beginning, practise making dome or boat-shaped pieces of simple icing lace work—similar to a trellis—over patty tins, small egg poacher pans, or boat-shaped tins. Later, use the shape of a cream horn tin, a serviette ring, or the side of a cocoa tin.

Before beginning to work, grease the outside of the mould thoroughly with lard or cooking fat. Grease the edges particularly well. Using a number one nozzle or tube in a paper bag, and well-beaten royal icing, pipe a single line of icing round the base of the mould, over the grease, to give strength and to act as a guiding line. Make a second line right over the centre of the mould, from the guiding line at one side, to the guiding line at the other side, dividing the mould in half. Continue making lines a quarter of an inch apart, parallel to the central line, right across the mould (diag. 71).

When these lines are completed, begin making lines across to form a trellis, either at right angles, to give small squares, or at an angle of 45°, to give a diamond pattern. If extra strength is needed, add a third row of lines, varying the pattern by cutting through the squares or diamonds already made. Finally, again to give added strength, make a thicker rim round the edge of the lace work, using the same number one tube, and piping a whipped line using a series of "*e*"-shaped twists. Put the worked moulds in a dry, warm place for several days before removing the set icing.

If any mistakes occur, and the icing is scraped off the mould, it will be necessary to grease the mould again. The discarded icing must on no account be put back into the bowl, as the grease in it would spoil the clean, unused icing.

When the icing is quite dry, place the mould in the left hand, with the icing side down against the hand, supporting it gently by cupping the fingers lightly round the mould. Now carefully pour hot water from the spout of a good pouring kettle, until it nearly fills the mould. The heat will melt the fat, a tiny tinkling noise will be heard, and with care, the mould full of water can be lifted from the icing, leaving the rounded trellis in the hand. Carefully lift by the edge, and place in a box on a bed of cotton wadding.

These lace domes can be used on formal, highly decorative cakes, particularly wedding cakes (pl. *59*), or even more effectively, by placing something under the raised trellis cage: a sprig of marzipan holly at Christmas-time, small piped flowers, or a silver shoe, shown in the picture of a silver wedding cake, plate *60*.

As a change from the trellis effect, make

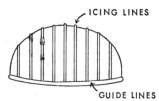

ICING LINES

GUIDE LINES

diag. 71

97. *Centre right*—Cake covered with pastillage to form a wheelbarrow and filled with marzipan roses—a birthday cake for a gardener.

99. *Bottom right*—A piped blue ribbon and roses in a trellis vase decorate the front of a pastillage birthday card which can be opened.

96. *Above*—Christmas cake decorated with gum paste holly and flowers and a book with gilded edges.

98. *Above*—A pastillage wheelbarrow and greetings tag and one rose for every year of a seasoned gardener's life.

100. *Top left*—Christmas cake using the plaque shown in colour on pl. **20**.

101. *Top right*—A royal icing woodpecker in brilliant orange, red and blue, perched on a branch of apple blossom —build up the body of the bird with over-piping. Work on waxed paper over a picture as in pl. *102*.

102. *Centre left*—A poodle on a glacé iced cake, while a second dog looks on. These animals are piped straight on to waxed paper placed over the picture, using the same method as in pl. **24**. When dry remove the waxed paper carefully and place the animal on the cake.

103. *Below*—Picture cake iced free-hand from an icing bag and painted with an artist's brush in edible colouring.

104. *Below*—A square cake with a raised net dome covering the central painted plaque.

106. *Below*—Making run-out flowers: on the glass sheet are stages in the formation of a wild rose, several ivy leaves, Christmas roses and narcissi.

105. *Above*—Pure white pastillage roses decorate a two-tier wedding cake.

107. *Left*—Run-out ivy leaves decorate a cake iced with cold fondant.

108. Run-out figures, clothes and limbs defined by outlining each section separately, filling with soft run-out sugar, and allowing each section to dry before the next one is filled.

109. Experimenting with run-outs: mauve pansies, a teddy bear and a dainty lace butterfly.

110. The perfect birthday cake for a six-year-old ballet dancer: the figure must be run-out on both sides.

111. A royal iced 'welcome home' cake decorated with a pale green raised centre run-out and a border of narcissi and half narcissi.

a lace pattern piping a design from the letters S, C and X. As before, the mould must first be greased on the outside, and a single line of icing piped round the edge of the mould, using a number one tube.

This time, fill the centre with these three letters, all touching each other, filling the whole surface of the mould and joining the edge. Letters must all be made touching each other (diag. 72). If there are any pieces not joined, the icing lace will break when it is taken from the mould. If any small spaces are found between the letters when the icing is completed, a small dot can be used to

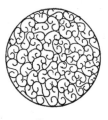

diag. 72

make the join. Finally, strengthen with a whipped edge or line of letter "e". Remove from the mould with hot water as before, and store in a warm dry place, in a box with wadding.

Keep a store of these filigree domes, and use them on the centre of a glacé or water-iced cake for quick effect. Do not keep too long on glacé icing, as the dampness tends to make the dome collapse if the cake is kept for several hours or overnight. It is preferable to put the decoration on glacé icing only just before serving, and to use the cake the same day.

TO MAKE A BASKET

Make a fine trellis or lace work basket to hold flowers by following the same method on a suitably shaped mould: it is possible to buy these in pink plastic. To work a

trellis on a mould with the top outer rim wider than the bottom outer rim, it is advisable to work sloping lines each side, and then to fill in the quarter lines to ensure that the remaining spaces are even. The lines at the top will naturally be a little wider apart than those at the bottom.

The lace pattern is far easier to work on this type of mould, but remember to strengthen the edge with tiny stars or whipping, and then leave to dry.

A garden trug basket can be made on the side of a cocoa tin, using the length and half the width round for the main part of the basket, and half the round top and bottom of the tin for the ends of the basket. Leave the three separate pieces to dry, and then fix together. Many different shaped ornaments can be made and fastened together in this way (pl. 62).

Making a handle for the basket

Grease a similar shaped mould, the correct size for a handle to fit the basket. Work two lines over the greased mould, and join with criss-cross trellis or lace work using the usual letters: X, C and S. When quite dry, remove the mould if possible using the hot water method, and if not, holding the icing handle near to a fire and supporting it in the hand until the grease melts and the icing can be carefully taken from the mould. It is advisable to make several spare handles when doing this fine work, as breakages are frequent.

To assemble the basket, fill the bottom with a little cotton wadding and top up with tiny sugar flowers or almond paste fruits. Put a star of icing on each side of the top of the basket, and carefully place the handle in position. Support with screwed up tissue-paper until the join is dry and firm.

These baskets can be used as a centre-piece for a birthday cake, and the lace work varied by colouring the icing. Using the same method, make a small trellis or lace work cradle (pl. 62). Work half the mould to make the cradle hood. Fix to one end of the complete basket shape, to resemble the cradle.

E

A LACE TRIANGLE CAKE
(pls. *63–67*)

Cut out a circle of greaseproof paper the same size as the cake top, using the baking-tin as a guide, or measuring the cake across and using a pair of compasses to make the circle. Divide the circle into the number of pieces of lace work needed—eight is preferable because it is easy (pls. *63* and *65*), although in plate *64* the cake had to be divided into nine portions, as the letters of *Christmas* were run into the centres of the pieces of lace.

Cut out the sections of paper carefully, and put onto a piece of glass, fastening the corners with a very little icing from a tube. Cover the sections with triangular pieces of thin waxed paper a little bigger than the greaseproof triangles which should show through the waxed paper. Again, fasten down at the corners with a little icing and outline each piece of greaseproof showing through the wax paper with a number one tube. Fill the centres of each of these triangles with the letters X, C and S (pl. *64*), or with zigzag lace work (pl. *65*). Also make small triangles for the edges of the cake having the base of each either equal to the top triangles, or half their size. Here again, make a few extra in case of breakages. Leave all the triangles until completely dry.

To remove the lace, place over the edge of a book or a box edge, and carefully bring the waxed paper downwards peeling it away from the icing.

A cake suitable for this type of decoration should have a plain, flat surface in white or coloured royal or cold fondant icing. As there is so much work involved in decorating this cake, use a good fruit cake that will keep well. Tie a ribbon or silver braid round the cake, or use decorative piping. Roll a ball of cold fondant icing into an inch wide marble shape, or if royal icing is used, add enough sugar to make a very stiff mixture, and roll into a ball, leaving on waxed paper to dry.

When dry, place the ball, or any other suitable ornament in the centre of the cake,

and place the large triangles carefully balancing between the cake edge and the ball, pointing in to the centre. Pipe a row of royal icing stars round the edge of the cake, seven or eight at a time. Place the small triangle in the soft stars, pointing downwards and outwards, one or two to every large top triangle. Similarly, pipe a row of stars round the bottom edge of the cake, again only piping seven or eight at a time, and put in small triangles opposite each of the top edge triangles, raised a little, not resting flat on the board (pl. *63*). For the design using two small triangles to one large one (pl. *64*), put in a row of triangles round the bottom edge opposite those round the top edge, and a second row nearer the board, but still raised slightly from the board. Study plate *64* as a guide: fifty-four small triangles are used.

Although it is always wise to follow the advice given earlier, and make a few extra triangles, it is amazing how few breakages actually occur once experience has been gained.

THE LACE TRELLIS COLLAR CAKE
(pl. *68*)

To make the collar

A pair of compasses and a sheet of perfectly smooth greaseproof paper will be needed if this circular sugar lace trellis is to be worked accurately. There must be absolutely no creases or fold marks in the greaseproof.

Draw a circle on the paper, the diameter of which is one inch greater than the diameter of the cake and a second circle inside the first, one inch less than the diameter of the cake. This will give a collar an inch wide all round, which will jut half an inch over the outer edge of the cake, and will be supported by the half inch overlapping the cake. If compasses are not available, two suitable sized plates can be used.

Mark dots a quarter of an inch apart round the inside of the greaseproof paper ring. Directly opposite one of these dots, mark a corresponding dot just inside the outer circle. Repeat on the opposite side of the outer circle, and at quarter positions, and then fill in dots evenly spaced on the outside circle until there is one corresponding to each one on the inner circle although naturally those on the outer circle will be spaced farther apart. Fasten the paper ring onto a piece of glass with a little icing, and cover with a smooth sheet of thin waxed paper. The waxed paper should also be fastened with dabs of icing.

Using a number one tube and well-beaten royal icing, pipe a line from a dot on the inner circle to a dot five away on the outer circle (point 1 to point E on diagram 73). Ice a second line, beginning on the inner circle at point 5, directly opposite point E, and joining point 5 to point A on the outer circle. This makes a start, the lines crossing in the middle. Continue making lines next to each other, following alternately the first line made, and then the second line made, until the circle is completed. The finish of the work will join up neatly, but it will always be visible: it can be seen on the left of the photograph, plate 68.

Finishing the cake

Complete the decoration on the cake before adding the lace collar, by making dainty poinsettias in almond paste or cold fondant coloured red. Make green leaves from the same material and mark with a knife or skewer. Add a few pieces of asparagus fern, and pipe yellow icing in the centre of the poinsettias for a realistic effect. Place a small flower and some fern on the sides of the cake, and small red florets at intervals on the board round the base. Circle the top edge of the cake with a narrow red ribbon.

Completing the board

Mark out the base of the cake and the cake board with dots in the same way as the greaseproof ring was marked for the top collar. Ice a trellis following the same directions. The dots on the cake should be about half an inch up the side of the cake. Touch the cake first with the tube, and bring the line of icing out long enough to reach the dots on the board, and then finish off. The hanging curve of icing must be the same length each time. This needs a

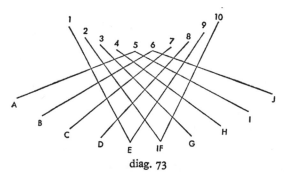

diag. 73

When the trellis lines are completed, add a row of dots close together round the inner circle for neatening and strengthening. Leave the work in a warm place for several days until quite dry. Remove the waxed paper very gently and carefully by peeling from the back of the lace work, the majority of the ring resting on the edge of a table. Work off a little at a time so that the waxed paper is removed only very slowly.

little practice before it can be carried out successfully. Neaten the lines of trellis with dots of icing.

Final stage

When the decoration on the cake has reached this point, lift the trellis collar very carefully from the paper onto the cake. Secure here and there on the inner edge with tiny dots of icing. Finally, add tiny hanging loops on the collar edge as seen in the photograph.

A LACE TRELLIS TOP FOR A CAKE
(pl. 69)

The particular cake photographed for this book, plate 69, uses five pieces of sugar trellis, worked in pale-blue. Before attempting to begin, the design must be worked out on greaseproof to ensure absolute accuracy. Using a pair of compasses, divide the circumference of a circle of greaseproof paper the same size as the cake, into five equal sections, marking each with a dot. Freehand, draw in the design shown in the photograph. Cut the pattern into five pieces which should all be the same, and shaped as diagram 74.

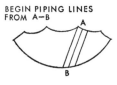

BEGIN PIPING LINES
FROM A–B

diag. 74

Place these five greaseproof paper patterns on a piece of glass, cover with slightly larger pieces of waxed paper, and fasten down at the corners with a dab of icing. Make sure that these dots of icing will not come under the trellis work.

Outline the shape of the five pieces with a number one tube, and begin working from the top right-hand point to the outer edge directly opposite the top left-hand point (diag. 74). Continue working lines parallel to each other, and one-eighth of an inch apart, working across the pattern from right to left. When this is completed, work the trellis by making lines in the opposite way, from left to right. Complete the five pieces, strengthening the inside edges with dots placed close together. Make one or two extra patterns in case of breakage. Leave these pieces to dry well in a warm place.

To complete the cake ready for the trellis work decoration, the top should be a good flat smooth surface of icing, and the sides should have a narrow band of deep-blue ribbon round the centre, and two narrow bands of silver paper braid cut to the right width and placed each side of the ribbon. Make about five deep-blue forget-me-nots using a petal tube and icing to match the deep-blue ribbon. Place these on the centre of the cake with dainty sprigs of asparagus fern. Fasten in position with a little icing from the tube.

Remove the pale-blue trellis from the waxed paper by peeling it away over the edge of a book. Place it in position on the cake over small stars or dots of icing placed at the corner positions to raise the trellis a little from the cake.

Using white royal icing and a large star tube, make long scrolls, starting thick in the middle of each of the five patterns, and gradually thinning out at the points where one piece joins the next. Neaten the join with a large star and with three graduated stars underneath it, extending over the silver band round the side of the cake. Repeat these same long scrolls on the board at the base of the cake and continue the stars at each join with three graduated stars out onto the board. The cake in the photograph is finished with a pale-blue edging of frilling round the board. This is optional, of course, but it gives a delightful finish to a very dainty cake.

A BALLET DANCER CAKE (pl. 72)

Preparation

Use a plain white royal iced cake. The board should also be iced in plain white. The lace work on the side of the cake is done in white royal icing, and can be worked on a smooth curved surface: a rolling-pin or a small jar or round bottle. The lace round the top of the cake can be worked on half a domed surface like an egg poacher and the small pieces of lace work can be made on greaseproof half circles drawn round a penny or an egg cup.

Before beginning to work, choose suitable moulds and see that their sizes are correct in relation to each other. Each piece of lace work must be made onto waxed paper before transferring to the cake.

Make eight pieces of lace work for the side of the cake, using the half circle of a bottle or rolling-pin to the height of the cake. Pipe straight onto a greased surface, use double waxed paper, or line the waxed paper with greaseproof, as the icing may seep through the paper and stick to the mould, causing the lace work to break when removed. Next, ice eight half-dome shapes, piping the lace work straight onto the greased surface of the mould, as it is not possible to cover the domed shape. When the work is completely dry, remove in the usual way either by gently pulling away the waxed paper from the icing, or by holding near a fire or the cooker, until the icing comes easily away from the mould. Make sixteen half circles in lace work with a diameter half the depth of the cake, and about sixteen further half circles, large enough to circle the edge of the board. To do this, measure the circumference of the board with a tape measure, and divide suitably to ascertain the measurement of the diameter of these half circles. Lastly, make a small triangular piece for the sundial centre.

Needless to say, it is sensible to make several spare pieces.

The pattern

Outline each shape first, using a number one tube and royal icing. Work a lacy pattern of regular shaped loops hanging one below the other, and finish with picot dots round the edge. New ideas for piping lacy patterns can often be found from crochet and knitting books, paper doyleys, and real lace.

Making the ballet dancers

These tiny figures are run-out—a method described in Chapter Fourteen. Four are made in pale-pink or flesh colour, and four in pale-blue. Make one or two more of each colour in case of breakage. Decorate the pink dancers with frills of

blue icing, and *vice versa*, using a number nought or double nought tube or a finely-cut bag for a dainty effect. The run-out figures must be quite dry before decorating. Use white royal icing and the fine tube, make lines for hair and shoes, and tint the hair and face suitably using edible colour and a fine artist's brush. Make dots for eyes and complete the faces.

Making the sundial

Use a roll of cold fondant to represent the sundial. Roll out a further piece of cold fondant to a quarter of an inch thick, and cut out an octagonal shape for the base of the sundial. Decorate the sides of the roll with the same loop design used on the lace, and place the triangular piece on the flat top surface. Stand the completed sundial on the octagonal base and neaten the join with dots. Secure in position on the cake with a little icing, using a small star to neaten the base.

Arrange two pink and two blue ballet dancers alternately, round the sundial, and the other four alternately round the sides of the cake, as it will be impossible to fix these later without breaking the lace work. Secure each dancer with a little icing from the tube.

Fixing the lace work

Leave the lace work for two or three days in a warm room to make sure that it has completely dried out.

Begin by fixing two domes opposite each other, and then filling in the others, to ensure even spacing. Fasten by making a row of stars round the top of the cake, only piping nine or ten at a time: just enough to fasten one lace dome. When these are completed, using a number one tube, make a double loop of hanging dots on the side of the cake under each alternate dome, over the ballet dancers. Neaten the top edge of the cake with stars, again only making nine or ten at a time, and fixing the large curved pieces of lace work, two at a time, round the side of the cake. Use the same method of fixing opposite sides first to even the spacing. Complete the top row of stars, and add another row round the base of the cake, and round the lace curves. Lastly, add stars up the side of the curves where the half circles are to be placed, and fix these in position two at a time, before making the next row of stars. Refer to the photograph as a guide.

Completing the board

Arrange the remaining half circles round the edge of the board, placing opposites and quarters first, and filling in evenly. Fasten in position with a final row of stars. Complete the board with a picot edge of dots. These knock off so easily that it is advisable to have a bag of icing ready to add the dots after the cake has been arranged in its final position. Even in this photograph it will be seen that in spite of great care one or two dots are missing.

To give a really splendid finish to this very ornate cake, make eight birds as described earlier in this book. Complete on waxed paper, and place between the half domes on the top edge of the cake.

THE "CUSHION" (*seen in* pls. *73–75*)

"Cushions" are a different form of raised work, used on the edges of either square or round cakes. The lines are built up on each other, beginning with three small lines in the centre, then three more crossing the first at an angle of 45°. Continue in this way, working over the first three lines and making an extra line at each side, and then working over the second three lines, adding an extra line each side (diag. 75). Work first one way and then the other, each time over-piping

the original lines and adding two new lines, aiming at an oval shape. If necessary, put a guide line over the edge of the cake before starting. The trellis lines are worked exactly over each other as the building up progresses, so that the cake can always be seen through the lines. This is very effective worked in colour, as the number of lines worked over each other appear to deepen the colour at the centre of the cushion.

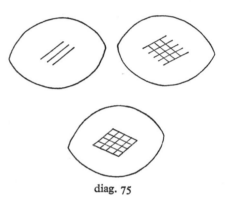

diag. 75

This work needs much practice, and should always be carried out on the edge of a practice board before working on the actual cake. It is not so easily broken as work done over a greased mould, and it is very suitable placed over the edge of a cake where a dome shape cannot be used, As the work proceeds, it may be necessary to tidy up the edges with a knife, as a good shape is most important. Neaten the finished cushion with a row of tiny stars or a piped line.

Part Two

CHAPTER THIRTEEN

Pastillage Work

There is far more scope in the art of sugarcraft than simply icing and decorating cakes. Pastillage work opens up a completely new dimension. Ornaments can be piped. Baskets can be made to hold marzipan fruits or sugar flowers. Christmas cakes can be decorated with Christmas cards; christening cakes with storks and cradles; wedding cakes with white roses.

To make icing suitable for pastillage work, make up royal icing in the usual way, and then to a teacupful of icing add half a level teaspoonful of powdered tragacanth. The best quality tragacanth can be bought from the chemist, and adds strength to icing. Stir in the powder, and allow to stand for at least an hour, or preferably overnight. Keep covered with a damp cloth.

TRAGACANTH BASKETS
(pls. *93* and **18**)

Grease the outside of a small mould—e.g. a ramikin dish—generously with lard or cooking fat. Make particularly sure that the edges are well greased. Using a large paper icing bag, tragacanth strengthened royal icing, and a number five star tube, pipe lines about half an inch apart across the base to the edge of the mould. Cross these lines either diagonally or at right angles (diag. 76).

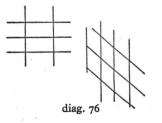

diag. 76

Turn the mould upside down, and with the base at the top, make hanging loops round the outside of the mould, leaving an inch between the ends. The second loop should overlap the first, as in diagram 77. Continue making overlapping loops in this way, so that the distance between the ends is now half an inch, until the last loop is completed. In the diagram, the last two loops would be placed from 7 to 1, and from 8 to 3. Make a ring of icing round the base of the mould with the star tube, neatening the loop ends. Leave for several days to dry in a warm, heated room.

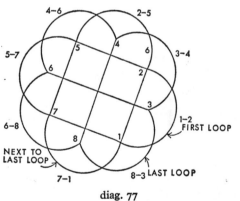

diag. 77

If necessary, make a handle for the basket by piping a line over the centre of the outside of a similar shaped greased mould. Either work a straight line, or a plait (diagram 78). Avoid making a plait too thick, although the edges must touch each other.

When both the basket and the handle are quite dry, remove from the mould. Hold the icing in the hollow of the left hand, supported by the fingers. Carefully pour hot water from the kettle into the mould. This melts the fat, and the tinkling noise will be heard. Lift the mould from the sugar basket. Take care over this,

diag. 78

particularly when removing the handle. In both cases, avoid allowing the water to run down the sides of the mould, as it would immediately melt the icing and cause it to break.

To complete the basket

Fill with marzipan fruits (*see* Chapter Four), sweets or chocolates, or arrange with ferns and marzipan flowers. Make two stars opposite each other on the edge of the basket, and place the handle in position. Support with tissue-paper until quite firm and dry. Do not attempt to lift the basket by the handle. Store in a dry place until required.

SUGAR DISHES AS A DINNER SWEET

Make sugar baskets as described above, some in white icing, and some coloured and flavoured with vanilla essence or peppermint, etc. Do not make any handles. Have some firm ice-cream ready in the refrigerator, and the sugar baskets ready on plates, and when the first courses of the dinner have been eaten, quickly cut the block of ice-cream into pieces, slipping one into each sugar dish. Top with a cherry or a sugar flower. This makes a specially unusual dinner party sweet.

When using the baskets in this way, do not attempt to make handles, as they would not set in place in time. If preferred, these baskets can be made without adding the tragacanth to the royal icing. If this is done, the baskets will not be so hard, but

very great care will need to be taken handling and filling them.

EDIBLE CHRISTMAS CARDS AND PLAQUES IN PASTILLAGE
(pls. *95* and *99*)

An edible Christmas card is a unique gift, and fascinating to make. The royal icing should be well beaten, and again, add half a level teaspoonful of powdered tragacanth to one teacupful of icing. Leave to stand overnight. Mix well, and add as much sifted icing sugar as can be absorbed. Knead well, using a little cornflour on the hands to prevent the mixture sticking. Lightly dredge the board and rolling-pin with cornflour, and begin to roll out the mixture now known as pastillage, also called gum paste. Roll out a piece evenly to about an eighth of an inch in thickness, and using a ruler as a guide, cut into two equal oblongs. Place on a sheet of glass evenly dredged with cornflour to prevent sticking.

With a large plain tube about number four, cut two holes in the sides of each sheet of pastillage, ready to take the Christmas card ribbon. Work quickly, or the pastillage will set and be cracked.

Any pieces not used should be kept under a cloth while working on another section, and the remaining pieces can be kneaded again, rolled out, and cut into round plaques with a biscuit cutter. Never waste any pastillage. Every little piece can be utilized. Small pieces make useful plaques for birthday cakes or for hanging on a Christmas tree, painted with a design in edible colours or flavoured with peppermint or even cough mixture and cut into lozenges or small "dolly mixture" sweets. Put messages on larger ones, and use them as a Hallowe'en novelty.

Making the picture on a sugar or pastillage card

If the worker is an artist there will be no difficulty in using edible colours to paint a picture or design freehand onto a sugar Christmas or Easter card or plaque. For the many people who are not artists, a simple tracing method can be used.

Find a card or picture in a book, the right size for use on the pastillage. Make a tracing on greaseproof paper and then outline the tracing on the back of the greaseproof, using graphite or black lead pencil. These are not harmful if eaten—never use Biro or copying ink. Place the tracing on the sugar card or plaque, pressing only lightly on the sheet or the gum paste will break. It is important to make sure that the sugar card is completely dry and flat. Outline the tracing again, remove the paper, and a fine outline should remain on the sugar. Colour in the picture with a fine artist's brush and a little edible colour, mixing the colours to the right shade. There is rarely any need to buy more than the three primary colours, yellow, blue and red, as a mixture of these will produce any other colour that may be needed, blue and yellow making green, blue and red making purple, yellow and red making orange, and all three mixed to varying degrees forming black and browns. To make the colours a lighter shade, simply add more water. It is advisable to try out a colour first on a small piece of gum paste before beginning a large important piece of work.

Never worry about making an exact copy of the original picture. This is not always possible on sugar, and perhaps this is a good thing. A very good effect can be achieved, and when after some time, the original has been forgotten and the sugar picture is studied again, the result is often more pleasing than a perfectly exact copy. Quite often a latent talent is discovered in this way.

For the best results, use a fairly dry brush for painting on the edible colouring. A wet brush is liable to melt the sugar surface which then becomes sticky. This technique becomes a lot easier with more practice.

To complete the Christmas card (pl. 95)

Write some simple greetings on the second piece of prepared pastillage, place the picture piece on top, and thread a piece of fine ribbon through the holes. Tie in a neat but loose bow, otherwise the card cannot be opened. Arrange in a suitable sized box lined with a thin piece of wadding, or use as a centre piece on a cake.

A PASTILLAGE BOOK
(pls. *96* and **20**)

A small book can quite easily be made by rolling out the pastillage to the size needed, and drying over a slightly rounded surface: a rolling pin or a jar dusted with cornflour. Rub the pastillage gently with a little cornflour on the finger, leave for a day or two to dry, and then brush away any surplus cornflour before beginning to colour in a picture.

Take special care tracing a picture onto the curved surface, or the gum paste will break. Press only very lightly, or support the book from underneath. Using a fine artist's brush, as before, only lightly dampened with edible colour, write suitable wording on one side of the pastillage page and paint a small design or picture on the other (pl. *96*). If the book is to be used on a cake, place in position fixed by a little royal icing underneath.

SUGAR PLATES AND DISHES
(pls. **21–23**)

Make these by combining the methods of making a plaque and those of making a sugar basket. Complete a gum paste plaque as explained previously, and when it is dry, paint a picture on it in edible colouring. Place on a china plate, fancy dish or mould, with cornflour and a strip of waxed paper underneath so that it is easier to lift later. Grease the uncovered outer edges of the plate or dish and pipe a lace work design from the plaque, making sure the icing joins onto the edge of the plaque. Add some tragacanth to this particular icing used for the piping to give extra strength.

Remove the sugar plate by warming gently over the flame of a gas cooker or a red fire, and slipping carefully off the mould. Arrange two or three marzipan fruits or chocolates on the plate, and use as a table decoration or a party novelty.

SUGAR BOXES

For the prettiest effect, make these from coloured pastillage, by kneading in some colour thoroughly, or using coloured icing to make the pastillage. Blue is perhaps the most attractive, as boxes of blue pastillage can easily be made to resemble Wedgwood china (pl. 23).

Cut paper patterns for complete accuracy. Make four for the sides of the box, one to fit in as a base, and one for the lid. If necessary, make patterns for lid edges at the same time. Sprinkle the board with cornflour, roll out the coloured pastillage to an eighth of an inch thick, and place the paper pattern on the paste, working quickly so that the pastillage does not set before the pattern is removed. Cut round the patterns with a sharp pointed knife, place the pieces on glass dredged with cornflour, and leave until quite set.

Using a number one tube and white or coloured royal icing, decorate the pieces of pastillage with designs of trellis, hanging loops, or polka dots. Again, leave to dry thoroughly, and then put the box together. Begin by fixing two opposite ends of the box to the base, using royal icing from the tube, and standing on cornflour until quite dry, propped with tissue-paper or a jam jar. When dry, fix the second two sides in position in the same way. The lid should be left until last, and can be separate, or fixed with icing to the box at an attractive half-open angle. When Chapter Fourteen has been studied, small run-out Wedgwood figures can be made to decorate the box—this medium can also be used for any small ornaments: toy engines, cradles, figures and animals. Pastillage was also used for the wheelbarrow cake (pls. 97 and 98), the pieces cut to shape and arranged round the cake with royal icing.

RAISED SURFACES
ON PLAQUES AND CARDS

Sometimes a second small plaque can be placed on top of a larger plaque to give a raised surface (pl. 95). In this case, the second plaque should be made as thinly as possible, so that the sugar is not too hard to eat—if any of these sugar novelties are a little hard, steam from a boiling kettle, or a short time in a damp place will soon soften the icing. It is often advisable to paint the second plaque only when it has been set in position, as the very lightest pressure could crack the thin pastillage if there is nothing to support it.

A figure can be outlined on pastillage and then filled with soft royal icing as in making ladies' fingers. When set, pipe in details of hair and features (pl. 108).

TO MAKE A BIRTHDAY CAKE
USING PASTILLAGE (pl. 99)

To prepare the cake

For this design, the edge of the cake must be well-angled with very little or no bevel. Measure the circumference of the cake, and work out the size needed for each trellis work circle—these should be made four large and four small, leaving an inch space between each one.

Draw the eight circles on thin cardboard with a pair of compasses. Cut through the centre, and place in position on the cake. Use as templates for icing both the top and the sides of the cake, the cardboard being held to the sides by a pin.

Pipe a line round the cardboard circles, and remove them from the cake. Next, using a number one tube, pipe the trellis, working lines parallel to the edge of the cake and when these are completed, crossing them at right angles over the side of the cake, beginning with a line from the middle of one top semi-circle to the middle of the semi-circle below. To do this successfully, it may be helpful to tilt the cake. Neaten the edges of the circles, and the edges of the cake in between the circles, with a small star tube.

The next step is to ice dots marking the position of the hanging loops. When the loops are complete, finish with five dots in each loop, and three dots between each loop. Lastly, work trellis lines over the whitened board, from the base of the cake to the board edge, working the lines all one way first, and then crossing with lines all going the other way. Remember that the outer edge of the board will be slightly wider than the inner edge, and a little bit of graduating will be needed. Neaten between the board and the cake with a row of small stars.

Making the birthday card

Roll out the gum paste as directed earlier in this chapter. Cut two pieces of a suitable size, and make small holes for the ribbon. Dry on glass sprinkled with cornflour. When the paste is completely set, pipe a small vase, using a number one icing tube. With practice, this can be done freehand. Fill in the vase with trellis lines, and neaten by outlining again. Using a ribbon tube, pipe a garland of pale-blue icing for the ribbon. When the garland is dry, write "Birthday Greetings" in deeper blue icing, using a fine nought or double nought tube. Make some tiny pink roses in two shades on a cocktail stick or a pin-head, allow to dry on waxed paper, and then place in position on the card face. Write a greeting inside the card, using pale-blue icing and a number nought tube, and tie the two pages of the card together loosely with blue silk ribbon to match the icing. Put a dab of icing on the back of the card and place in position.

Place a single rose between the slightly opened card to prevent the top page crushing the piped writing inside.

THE CHRISTMAS CAKE WITH PASTILLAGE PLAQUE (pl. *100*)

To make a picture of this type, take a tracing from a Christmas card, and trace out onto a plaque of gum paste, colouring as explained earlier. The plaque used in the centre of this particular Christmas cake is the same as the one shown earlier, in plate **20**.

Fold a circle of paper the same size as the cake surface into eight equal parts, mark out to an eight-point star, and then round off the inner edges. From this paper pattern, make a template. Place the template in the centre of the cake and work round it.

To make the trellis, begin by piping a line from the centre of each hollow, to the edge of the cake, and filling in with parallel lines. Cross these at right angles with lines beginning with a single line from one star point to the next. Complete the shape with two more curved lines outlining the pattern, building up the middle line once more, and the outer line three times. Place the plaque in position, a little to the top, leaving room to write greetings below. Arrange a ring of marzipan holly round the plaque.

Finish by making hanging loops from point to point round the side of the cake, decorating with a lily pattern, and making a shell edge round the base of the cake and round the top edge, using a star tube, number five or larger if preferred.

A CAKE WITH A CENTRAL DOME (pl. *104*)

This is an interestingly designed cake, having the pastillage work half hidden in the centre under a lace work dome (for making, *see* Chapter Twelve). The plaque can be designed applicably for almost any event, showing a school badge, a message, greetings, or a picture of some particular season or event.

The basic design for the cake is the same as that used previously in the cake in plate *100*. Cut a thin cardboard template in the same way, and work the outer line of the design. Remove the template, and repeat the pattern line three times, making the middle line two rows deep, and the outer line three deep. Inside the inner pattern line, follow the design with a line of dots, adding eight short rows of dots from each point to the centre piece.

In the centre of each top edge, work a cushion, neatening each one with a shell edge. Put double hanging loops from each of the cushions, and add hanging dots between the loops. Tie a coloured ribbon round the centre of the cake. Make twelve roses on cocktail sticks, to match the colour of the ribbon, and add several pull-out leaves. When dry, arrange these in position at the corners. Arrange the plaque in position, with the lace dome placed over it. Hold the dome in position with an edging of shells.

Whiten the board with icing, and when dry, cover neatly with braiding and finish with a long scroll at the base of the cake. Two or three shells neaten the corners of a square cake.

FREEHAND PIPING ON PLAQUES
(pl. 24)

Some of the most delightful scenes involve animals (*see* pl. 24). These can be drawn freehand or traced onto a gum paste plaque which has been allowed to dry thoroughly. Once the basic outline has been transferred to the pastillage, begin to work on the detail.

Using a bag only and royal icing, cut to the size of a number one tube and used like a paint brush, make lines to represent the animal's hair. Work in white or coloured icing, choosing the palest colour on the animal, as the darker colours can be painted in with a brush. Work over the first row of icing to build up the body of the animal and give it shape. The photograph shown in plate 24 shows work in progress—no tube is used, as a bag gives a softer result. In this way, quite elaborate pictures can be built up using a number of bags of coloured icing at the same time. Obviously this comes more easily to anyone with an artistic tendency, but it is amazing what can be achieved by almost anyone, once the attempt has been made.

GUM PASTE OR PASTILLAGE FLOWERS

This medium is particularly good for making flowers, as it can be pressed out very thinly and sets quickly, so that the petals hold their shape well. Pastillage takes any colour well whereas flowers made with marzipan have to contend with the basic colouring of the almond paste, which often presents a problem when clear pinks are needed. Pastillage is especially indispensable for making pure white or very pale pink roses for wedding cakes.

Making white roses for a wedding cake
(pls. *59* and *105*)

Pastillage for roses is made up in exactly the same way as it is for making cards or plaques. Make a cone about three-quarters of an inch high, and half an inch wide at the base. Roll out a small piece of pastillage to an eighth of an inch in thickness, keeping the paste covered with a cloth, and cut only one small round at a time for each petal, using a sharp half-inch round cutter. If several are cut at a time, the edges of the petals will tend to crack. Thin out the circle of pastillage between the thumb and finger until it is paper thin. Using a little water on a fine brush to dampen the base of the petal, fold round the cone, completely enclosing it. Cut a second circle, and leaving the base thick, thin out the top of the petal with the thumb and finger. Dampen the thick base slightly with a brush and place at the back of the first petal. Continue adding as many petals as necessary, curling over the final petals slightly. Prop with tissue-paper to keep the shape. It is possible to produce a good effect with as few as four, five or six petals, in fact more should not really be needed. Work quickly as this paste soon becomes too hard to model.

It is always advisable, before trying to make good model roses, to look at some real roses in the garden, or at least some wax roses, or realistic pictures.

To make coloured roses (pl. *25*)
Knead a little colour into the pastillage,

and then follow the previous directions. Two-coloured roses can also be made by using a piece of white or pale-yellow and a piece of pink pastillage, both rolled out until about a quarter of an inch thick, and then placed on top of one another and rolled together until the paste is one-eighth of an inch thick, pink on one side, and white or yellow on the other. Cut out circles as if making ordinary white roses, and put together as before. Aim at making the finished flower suitably shaped for adding a few leaves at the back. Prop the roses with tissue-paper until quite dry.

To make Christmas roses (pls. *117* and *121*)

Roll out the pastillage as for the wedding cake roses and cut very small circles. Press out evenly all over, and prop up the petals on tissue-paper, curving them slightly. When dry, tint each petal very lightly with streaks of pale-pink or green at the base. Make a knob of icing on waxed paper, and insert five or six petals to form a flower. Have ready some stamens, made by piping lengths of pale-yellow or white with a number one tube onto waxed paper. Tip each stamen with a yellow dot, and using tweezers, place in the royal icing centre of the flowers while the icing is still wet. Prop with screws of tissue-paper.

Almost any other flower can be copied and modelled in pastillage—orchids, daffodils and carnations can be made to look especially realistic.

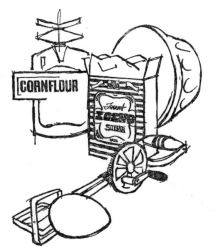

CHAPTER FOURTEEN

Run-out Work

(Soft Sugar or Run-in Work)

Although this type of decoration is immensely popular in exhibition work, it is still comparatively new. Cakes decorated with run-out look attractive, and smart: essentially modern. It is suitable for carrying out almost any idea—a visit to a trade exhibition and a glimpse of the effects achieved in this particular branch of sugarcraft will fire any student's ambition. With a little care, attractive decorations are produced, and though rather fragile for sale in shops, they are perfect for special occasion cakes.

Equipment and materials required

The best medium to work on is a piece of glass edged with sticky tape to prevent any accidents. Also needed: some waxed paper, greaseproof paper, a soft and a hard pencil, a soft good quality artist's paint brush, edible colours, a ruler, and, if wished, a pair of compasses.

The method

The basic principle used in this work is to outline the shape required, and then to fill in the centre with soft icing. Begin by attempting small pieces of work until used to handling the delicate pieces and working this new method. Then progress to larger run-outs. After a little practice, it is amazing how the large pieces stay intact in spite of handling.

Commencing the work

As a start, try making small, round plaques, natural-sized flowers, preferably spring flowers, or leaves (pl. *106*). Ivy leaves serve as a good beginning.

Find a suitably sized, well-shaped ivy leaf (diag. 84). Trace or copy this shape several times onto different pieces of smooth greaseproof paper—making all the leaves on one sheet of paper might result in breakages when they are removed. Using small dots of icing at each corner of the paper patterns, fasten down onto a sheet of glass. Cover each pattern with a square of waxed paper slightly larger than the greaseproof paper. Fasten with icing. Avoid allowing any icing under the actual tracing of the leaf.

Make some normal strength piping icing coloured light-green: this is preferable to a dark-green true ivy colour, as it is the idea that has to be conveyed, rather than an actual copy. Outline the leaf pattern on the waxed paper. There should be no breaks in the outline, which should be joined neatly at the points. Thin the remaining icing in the basin with a little water or albumen solution, stirring the mixture carefully. Avoid beating as this makes air bubbles which are difficult to remove. The consistency should be about that of un-whipped double cream, just thick enough to coat the back of a spoon, and the surplus from it to run back smoothly into the basin.

Using a teaspoon, fill the leaf outline carefully, or put the icing into a bag, cut equivalent to a number two tube and fill the leaf from the bag, going round the outside first and gradually filling in. This work should be carried out as quickly as possible, as the outer line should not be dry when the filling is put in, or it will show, and may break easily. Using a fine paint brush, move the icing round until the leaf is filled and no bubbles are showing. Any bubbles which do continue to rise must be pricked out with the brush or with a pin.

When completed, shake the sheet of

112. *Top left*—An eight point star pattern, decorated with trellis work between the points, surrounds another run-out Santa Claus.

113. *Top right*—Christening cake for twins, Rachel and Charlotte, the run-out stork and book over-piped with a fine tube to define pages and feathers.

114. *Centre right*—A barrel-organ scene, the cake cut to size, covered with run-out pieces and surrounded with run-out figures on a base of green coconut 'grass'.

115. *Bottom left*—Elaborate decoration for a table centre: swans and cygnets glide down a mirror lily pond while flying birds and kingfishers watch from a bank of green royal icing.

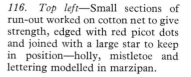

116. *Top left*—Small sections of run-out worked on cotton net to give strength, edged with red picot dots and joined with a large star to keep in position—holly, mistletoe and lettering modelled in marzipan.

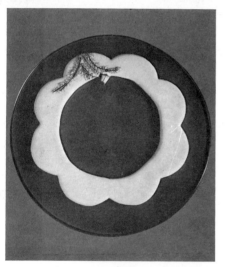

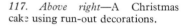

117. *Above right*—A Christmas cake using run-out decorations.

118. *Centre left*—A plain scalloped run-out collar completed on waxed paper and sheet glass before transferring to the cake; a lantern has been run in at the same time as the collar and fine green piped line fern added.

119. *Below*—A novel run-out birthday cake for a boy after winning a trophy at the swimming baths.

120. *Top right*—Christmas choirboys stand in rough icing snow round a simple white Christmas cake.

121. *Centre right*—A square Christmas cake decorated with square run-outs with the cake surface of pale green icing showing through. The sides of the cake are also run-out pieces. Pastillage is used for the Christmas roses.

122. *Centre left*—A pale pink cake for a 21st birthday, with run-out petals in the flowers and fine piped fern. Note: run-out on the board is raised.

123. *Bottom right*—Another Christmas cake decorated with a dainty scalloped collar.

124. *Top left*—A painted picture cake which can be copied or traced from the card shown on the right.

125. *Centre right*—Cake for a sailing enthusiast; a rough surface of pale blue icing represents waves supporting a pastillage yacht.

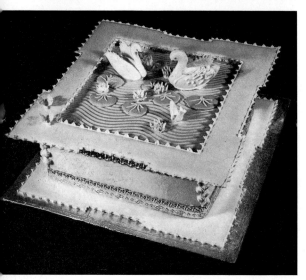

126. *Centre left*—A serrated scraper makes the smooth ripples on the pale blue surface of this 'lake'; swans and lilies should be placed in position after the run-out collar and butterflies.

127. *Bottom right*—Run-out icing sections made on cotton net to give strength. Fixed in position alternately with sprays of red roses and fern.

128. *Centre left*—A delicate birthday cake decorated with lace and run-out work, the top pieces worked first on waxed paper, those at the base of the cake worked straight on to the board. For this cake the surface must be perfectly smooth. Birds, pastillage roses, and bells worked on a mould complete the decoration.

129. *Top right*—Sugar lace and run-out work combined to edge a wedding cake, showing the three sizes for the top corner of each tier; lace work is shown in progress, the run-out is added later. See also Pl. *174*.

130. *Above.* A 'welcome' cake decorated with lace and run-out sections, and a plain run-out cake with a nest of eggs as the centre-piece, and a rabbit chasing a hen in a 'field' of daisies and buttercups.

131. *Above*—An imposing wedding cake for Michael and Anne, with their initials forming a run-out monogram; a double run-out decorates each tier, the lower one plain, the upper one patterned with lace and bells.

132. *Top*—Decorations taken from doily designs: place the doily on a flat surface, fasten with icing, cover with waxed paper and outline the design with a no. 1 tube, run in solid parts in white or colour, and over-pipe if necessary, as in the cake on the left. Only remove from the waxed paper when absolutely dry.

133. *Centre*—Dainty garden scene, the figures and tree flooded with run-out icing, the remainder piped. Several different patterns are used in the lace work collar.

134. *Bottom*—A plain run-out decorated with small lacy sections; the bridge is worked in sections and put together when dry.

135. *Top right*—An elaborate lacy run-out incorporating the delicate outline of a narcissus—this can be seen particularly clearly in the top right-hand flower—the grassy surface of the picture has been run-out on the cake; the rabbit, egg and chick made previously on waxed paper.

136. *Centre*—A double run-out, pink roses and silver shoes decorate a silver wedding cake.

137. *Bottom*—A double run-out suitable for any special occasion cake.

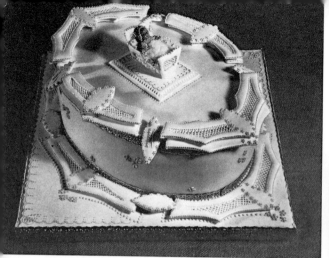

139. Centre right—Greetings cake decorated with lace and run-out lettering; anemones and maidenhair fern complete the centre.

138. Above—An elaborate christening cake, oval in shape, covered with pale cream cold fondant. Run-out shapes are edged with pale blue dots, and decorated with forget-me-nots. The bought doll in the run-out icing cradle wears an icing bonnet of blue dots and is covered with a net edged with icing lace.

141. Below—Snowdrops, pale green cold fondant and pale green run-out collars decorate a wintertime cake.

140. Centre left—An especially neat birthday cake with double run-out collars, and eight run-out and lace work sections round the sides giving an octagonal shape; pink piped roses and old English run-out lettering complete the design.

glass gently and bump it lightly on the table to make sure that all the icing is quite even and level. The leaves should be full and rounded, but not so full that they are liable to over-flow. If possible, place the sheet of leaves in front of an electric fire for a few seconds to set the surface, and then dry in a warm, heated room overnight, or even for two or three days. When quite dry, store the leaves in a tin, still on the waxed paper, packed between layers of wadding.

To remove the ivy leaves from waxed paper

Place the leaf over the edge of a thick book and peel the waxed paper gently downwards. Turn the leaf round, loosening the points first, and then holding the leaf gently in one hand, continue bringing the waxed paper down and away from the leaf with the other.

Use ivy leaves with piped flowers as a flower arrangement in the centre or round the edge of a cake (pl. *107*). As a finishing touch, pipe in a line to represent the vein of the leaf, and a line for the stem.

RUN-OUT NARCISSI AND DAFFODILS (pls. *106* and *111*)

Draw the pattern for a narcissus or daffodil flower freehand, or take a tracing from a picture card or a catalogue. The flower should be positioned as if looking straight into the trumpet (diag. 89). Make the tracings each onto a separate piece of paper—about twelve should be sufficient for an eight-inch cake. Fasten down to a sheet of glass with dots of icing, and cover with waxed paper, also fastened with icing.

Pipe the outline of the flowers with a number one or nought tube, making sure not to go into the centre. Fill the flower with soft icing: yellow for daffodils and white for narcissi, running in the icing smoothly, using a paint brush to spread evenly and remove any bubbles. The result looks like smooth white icing. Leave to dry in a warm place.

After about thirty-six hours, using a number nought tube in a bag with the same coloured icing in a piping line strength, outline the outside edges of alternate petals only. When this is done, outline the entire edges of the remaining petals from the centres to the outside edges. This gives the effect of the three outer petals opening first, and being outside the three inner petals, as they are in reality. Inside the petals, make a neat circle of icing with a number nought tube. Continue working this circle two or three times, until the trumpet is long enough. On the last time round, flute the edge a little. Leave the flowers until quite dry, and then paint the edge of the centre of narcissus trumpets with an orange colour, using an artist's paint brush. The brush should be almost dry or else the colour may spread down the trumpet and spoil the effect. Look through a bulb catalogue to find different varieties, making daffodils with yellow petals and white centres, or yellow petals with orange centres. There are so many variations that it is impossible to go wrong.

Decorating the narcissus cake (pl. *111*)

These flowers are intricate to make, and for this reason perhaps best used on special occasion cakes. Arrange as a spray with a few piped leaves, or use round the edge of a cake as a flower border. When using a flower border pattern, "half flowers" should also be repeated on the board. Cut in half the original traced paper pattern, and place the tracing on the silver board to the edge of the completed cake. Outline in pencil on the board. Outline again, on top of the pencil line, using royal icing in a number one or nought tube. Fill the half flowers with soft icing, and leave to dry. Take care to fit in a complete number of flowers, and to take the icing to the edge of the cake.

Leave until quite dry, and then pipe in the outline of the petals again, and half trumpets to match the full flowers. The half trumpets should be against the cake. Unless very great care is taken, the colour from yellow daffodils may seep up into the white icing on the cake. To cover this, fasten a narrow silver braid or ribbon just

F

at the base of the cake with icing (pl. *111*).

Completing the narcissus cake

Leave the completion of the top of the cake until last. Add any inscription or motif, and the half flowers round the base. Now, holding each flower carefully in the hand, draw off the waxed paper downwards, taking care not to force the paper or the flower may break. Turn the flower, loosening the edges of the petals first, and finally, the whole flower.

Make a rope of icing all round the top edge of the cake, using normal strength icing and a star tube. Place the loose flowers in the rope, exactly above the half flowers on the board—the petals should fit in so well that the icing rope is hidden. Alternatively, a star of icing can be put on to the back of each flower. Whichever method is used, the flower should be raised a little, and not lying flat. If necessary, add a series of stems, pull-out leaves or bought silver leaves between each flower to neaten, but if leaves are used towards the outside edge of the cake a similar row of leaves must be added to the flowers on the board, as they should be a reflection of the top row.

Marguerite daisies, yellow and orange marigolds, pink pyrethrums, pansies and other flat flowers can all be used in this way. The centre of the cake can be left plain, or hold greetings, a name, or a motif (pl. **26**), but too much decoration can spoil a cake. Flowers are shown up to their best advantage if the centre is left perfectly plain.

WILD ROSES (pl. *106*)

Trace a wild rose pattern from one of the cotton flowers sold in June on Alexandra Rose Day, a picture in a book, or draw one freehand. The best way to do this is to draw a circle the appropriate size, and to divide the circumference of the circle into five equal parts for the five petals. Make a dot in the centre of the circle, and draw in the petals (diag. 79). Using very light pencil, divide the circle into five equal

segments, joining the centre dot and the five points on the circumference. At the end of each division, make a small letter V, curved at the tops, and continue the curves, making a slight hollow in the centre of each petal. About twelve patterns will be needed for an eight-inch cake.

diag. 79

Cover the tracings with waxed paper and fasten down on glass (pl. *106*).

Have ready some pale-pink, rose-coloured royal icing, and some thinned out icing for the soft sugar work. Outline the petals of each flower at the edges only, not piping into the centres. Fill with the soft sugar run-out icing and prick out any bubbles. Leave until dry, and then outline the petals almost to the middle with a number one or nought tube. Thin out the line of icing, pulling it off towards the centre of the flower. The two lines of each petal should lie together. Finish the centre with a circle of yellow dots, or fine lines thinning out from the centre to resemble rays. Experiment to find the most suitable effect. For illustration of each step towards making the wild rose, *see* plate *106*.

To use these flowers as decoration on a rich fruit cake, cut the pattern in half and use similarly to the narcissus design, placing the half-flowers round the base of the cake. Arrange touching each other, outlining with pencil, piping over the pencil line and filling in, as before, with soft sugar. When set, pipe over the outline again to form petals and fill in the yellow half-centre. If a pink tinge creeps up into the white icing, cover with a length of narrow silver braid or ribbon. Arrange the finished wild roses round the top of the cake, exactly above the half-flowers on the board, and secure with a dab of icing. If necessary, add an inscription in the centre of the cake.

PANSIES (pl. *109*)

Make a tracing, using a method similar to that described in the making of a wild rose. Using yellow, white, or pale-mauve icing, outline the lower large petal in each flower onto waxed paper, fill with soft sugar, and leave to dry. When set, outline the two upper petals and fill with deeper yellow, deeper mauve, or white. When these are dry, complete one more petal on one side, and the final petal on the opposite side of the flower. By outlining and completing each petal separately, a distinctive effect is achieved, and two colours or shades can be put into the same flower.

To complete, when the icing is dry paint the pansy "face" in streaks of edible colour using a fine brush. Centre the flower with an elongated dot of green. Use in flower arrangements, or round the top and base of a cake on a surface of royal icing, cold fondant or sugar paste. Glacé icing is not suitable for use with these flowers, as the soft icing makes the flowers run.

LILIES (pl. *91*)

A curved piece of run-out is needed to make a good lily. Draw a suitably sized circle, divide into eight sections, and from this basic pattern make eight petals (diag. 80). Using the tracing, run out these petals flat onto waxed paper, and then before the icing is dry place them over a rolling-pin or a rounded tin to make a convex petal. For a concave petal, lay in a basin or a hollow round. Hold near the fire and rotate backwards and forwards for a few minutes until the surface of the icing is set. Leave for a day or two to become quite firm, and place in position on the cake, making a firm star of icing under the central point of the flower where all the petals meet. Prop in position with cotton wool or tissue-paper until quite set.

This decoration is a suitable ornament for the centre of the top tier of a wedding or christening cake—a tiny doll can be placed in the centre of the flower, if made large.

diag. 80

RUN-OUT RINGS

Rings can be made similarly to lily petals by placing an oblong strip of run-out icing three-quarters of the way round a suitably sized stick, making sure that the icing is slack enough to be removed when set. For safety, use double-waxed paper, as most run-outs are liable to make the waxed paper soft and stick to the mould.

Make lace strips or lace centres with run-out edges in the same way, flat on waxed paper, and quickly, while still soft, place round the curved surface. Alternatively, work the lace on a greased surface, perhaps a serviette ring, warming the ring by the fire to remove the icing.

Use these run-out rings on the edge of a cake, as if biting into the icing.

BLOSSOM PETALS (pls. *90* and *122*)

Use tiny heart shapes or pointed ovals, similar to lily petals. Have ready a suitably curved hollow tin or saucer, and two lots of icing—thin, soft sugar icing in pink and in white, and some softer than usual line piping icing. Make sure that the mould is well greased.

Pipe single petals onto separate pieces of waxed paper, place immediately into the mould, and, using a brush, fill with white soft sugar icing. With a second brush, fill in the base of the petal with pink soft icing. Take great care, as each petal should be thin and delicate. When all the petals are dry, store in a box until needed.

To assemble on the cake, pipe a branch in brown icing on the dry cake surface, and place the petals in position with tweezers, securing with a dot of icing piped on the cake. Prop with tissue-paper until dry. Finish the spray with green pull-out leaves, iced straight onto the branch. Pipe in stamens, or arrange previously made ones while the centre is still wet.

Use these petals to represent apple, peach, cherry, hawthorn, lilac, or any other blossom, according to size, colour and shape.

PIPING RUN-OUT FIGURES
(pls. *108* and *110*)

This method of icing run-outs can be used for producing all kinds of figures: animals, children skating, children dancing and skipping, nursery rhyme characters or ballet dancers. There is no end to the list of possibilities. The figure can be run out whole and then painted, or it can be run out in sections, forming divisions between clothing and limbs. One layer of icing can be run out on top of another, giving the effect of folds and thicknesses. The extent of variety will perhaps be emphasized by studying the figures decorating the cakes photographed in plates *108* to *110*, and *112* to *114*.

SWANS (pls. *115*, *126* and *134*)

Learning to make run-out swans is the next step in progression through this branch of cake decoration. Begin in the accepted way, by drawing a swan, or taking a tracing from a picture—a figure for tracing is included in the back of this book. The two wings should be made separately from the body and head of the bird. Following the same method used to make an ivy leaf, outline the swan, and the left and right wings by piping onto waxed paper. Fill with soft icing. Prick out the bubbles and leave to dry.

When the body of the swan is quite dry, turn it over and outline again on the actual icing. Fill in with soft icing. This step should not be repeated for the wings. Leave on waxed paper to dry and in the meantime, using a number one or nought tube, pipe in lines on the wings to represent feathers, working up towards the tail, leaving the breast ends of the wings quite smooth. Rub with the fingers to accentuate this smoothness.

When the body and head are quite dry, colour the beak with orange edible colour and put in the black seer with confectioner's black, a mixture of blue, red and brown edible colour, or a soft graphite pencil. Notice by studying a good picture of a swan, that this black marking is quite large, and the eye is almost a continuation. When the head is completed, make a bulb of icing each side of the body and place the wings in position. Prop with tissue-paper until set.

To make the scene in plate *115*, place the swans on a long mirror, and make run-out water lily leaves (diag. 83) and flowers (see page 77) to set off the picture.

CHAPTER FIFTEEN

Advanced Run-out Work

The scope of run-out work extends far beyond the decorations described in the previous chapter. This method can also be used to make an attractively shaped collar to surround a simple cake, lifting it from the ordinary to the special, and giving it a finished, tailor-made look.

Making a large circular or square run-out collar

Great care must be taken when making large run-outs. They are liable to break easily, and yet with a little care, it is amazing how much handling they will withstand. A run-out collar gives an excellent finish to a cake, tending to make a small cake look larger. A round cake should have a round collar and a square cake a square collar but perhaps to give an unusual design try placing a square collar on a round cake or *vice versa*.

The silver cake drum or thick board should be about four inches larger than the cake, according to the size of the run-out being used. This acts as a protection against breakages and adds to the appearance of the cake.

Measure the size of the cake with a ruler or tape measure. Making sure to leave a margin all round, draw the exact shape of the cake top onto a sheet of greaseproof paper. It is possible to take measurements from the baking-tin, but if thick layers of marzipan and icing have been used, these must be taken into account. From now on, the pencilled outline of the cake will be called the *cake line*. It may be helpful to write these words along this original line, to save any mistakes.

Outline the shape of the cake twice more, once on the outside and once on the inside of the cake line, making both lines half an inch from the cake line. This is all the pattern that is required to make a plain collar. To add a scalloped edge, use a pair of compasses to draw the scallops round the outer circle (diag. 81), or use the "folding paper" method (pls. *118* and *119*). For a large scallop design, or a deep bracket shape, the inner edge may be allowed slightly inside the half-inch line. Alternatively, scallops may also be put on the inside of the collar.

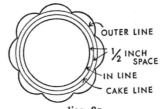

OUTER LINE
½ INCH SPACE
IN LINE
CAKE LINE

diag. 81

When the pattern is completed, cut out with scissors and fit over the cake to see if the whole effect is suitable and well-balanced. For good support the collar should over-lap the edge of the cake inside by half an inch all the way round.

Make a new perfectly smooth, clean pattern on fresh greaseproof paper by drawing round the original pattern—which must still be kept for use later on. Do not cut out the new pattern, as the edges can be used to fasten with a dab of icing onto the glass or with drawing pins onto a board. A large board or glass will be needed to make this large run-out—preferably glass, as it remains perfectly flat and does not absorb the liquid from the icing. Make absolutely sure that there is no icing and there are no drawing pins under the pattern of the actual collar. Cover tightly with thin, smooth waxed paper fastened down with a little icing at the corners.

Make the soft sugar or run-out icing by adding a little water or albumen solution to some well-beaten, normal strength icing until it is the consistency of un-whipped double cream. Do not beat when adding the liquid. Stir gently but thoroughly, scraping down any thick icing from the spoon or the sides of the basin so that the consistency is perfectly even. About a teacupful of soft icing is sufficient for an eight-inch run-out collar. Be careful to make enough icing before beginning the collar, as it dries quickly, and any join will show. Left-over soft icing can always be added to the original and re-beaten, adding more sugar if necessary, and perhaps a little more albumen to bring it up to strength. When the run-out icing is made, cover with a cloth and leave for a few minutes until the bubbles subside.

While the icing is standing, outline the design using piping strength icing and a number one tube. Break at any points in the design, and join again neatly, avoiding joins in a circular scallop. It is not easy to pipe right round the inner circle with only the one finishing join, but with practice and experience, and by lifting the icing slightly, it will soon become possible. While the soft outer line is still wet stir the run-out icing gently and then fill in the pattern with soft sugar run-out icing, using a teaspoon, or piping from a bag with a hole cut to a number two size. Work round the edge of the design first, so that it cannot become dry: a dried edge will show a line. For the same reason, work from each side of a large collar, so that the icing cannot dry in a ridge.

Use a fine brush for spreading the icing and removing any bubbles, and when the collar is finished, prick out any remaining bubbles, gently lift the sheet of glass, and bump it slightly on a table. This should level the icing. Again, prick out any bubbles that may have appeared, and leave the collar quite undisturbed for two or three days until completely dry. Placing about two feet away from an electric fire for a few minutes before leaving to dry should produce an attractive gloss.

One of the best places for drying these run-outs is a slightly heated airing cupboard, although the icing must not be left in this atmosphere for too long, or it will become yellow and discoloured. When the run-out is nearly dry and there is no risk of stickiness, protect from dust with a light cover of tissue-paper.

Completing the decoration on a run-out collar

Outlining the collar will give a bolder effect and add strength, but for pure decoration add a simple lace work edge of dots or tiny lines—this will also camouflage a bad edge. Decoration can be added in colour, although this is only for the more advanced student: white icing is less likely to show defects.

In the ready dried collar photographed in plate *118*, a lantern has been run-in at the same time as the collar was made. To add effect to this idea, over-pipe with piping strength icing, using a number one or nought tube. In this particular collar, fine green work represents evergreens round the lantern.

But although all these decorations are attractive and fascinating to work, a really good, well-made run-out collar is most effective absolutely plain.

Variations on the plain run-out collar

As an alternative to the collars already described, cut-out spaces can be left and filled in with net work similar to the trellis and lace work shown earlier in this book. For a 21st birthday cake, the number "21" can be incorporated in the run-out, or perhaps some initials. These must first be planned in the original pattern, drawn carefully to scale, and outlined at the same time as the collar itself. In this case, use the soft icing in a bag for filling, as it is difficult to flood the small spaces between the letters, and if the edge line breaks, the whole design will probably have to be started all over again.

Putting the run-out pattern onto the board

When the cake is made and completed with a good dry surface, a reflection of the run-out collar pattern should be made on the cake board round the base of the cake.

Take the first paper pattern made and cut along the cake line. Cut the pattern in half, and place the two halves to meet round the base of the cake, if necessary cutting a little more paper away to ensure a good fit. Fasten down lightly with a little icing. Pencil round the pattern, and remove the paper.

Using piping icing and a number one tube, pipe round the outline slightly on the outer side, so that no pencil mark can be seen when the design is filled. Have the soft sugar ready, and fill in the space between the outline and the cake. If there are no cut-out spaces, spread with a fine artists' brush or a teaspoon. For a design with spaces, use a piping bag to fill in the soft sugar. Make sure that the icing flows neatly to the base of the cake, particularly if coloured run-out is being used. Any lacy work should be done before the soft sugar is put in.

When the board work is dry, complete the picot edge, and any other decoration to the cake except standing ornaments. If necessary, add a silver braid or decorative ribbon.

Removing the collar from the waxed paper

This is very difficult, and often leads to disappointment. The only approach is to be pleased when the collar comes off intact, rather than despondent when it breaks. Any arrangements of previously piped flowers should be put onto the collar before it is removed from the wax, making sure that all the decoration is firmly attached to the icing collar.

Place the run-out to the edge of a table or flat upturned tray, and very carefully peel off the waxed paper downwards. Turn the collar frequently, loosening round the edges first and then gradually working to the middle. When the entire collar is quite loose, work any picot dots to correspond with the collar on the board, and when quite dry, re-loosen the run-out. Some of the picot edge may break off, but can be replaced either immediately, or when the collar is on the cake. If a trellis or lines are planned for behind the collar, turn it over very carefully, and using a

stiff icing, pipe in the trellis lines right across the back over the farthest edges of the cut-outs. The lines should be taut and not sagging. For this reason work the trellis the shortest distance across the open cut-out (pl. *138*).

To fasten the collar to the top of the cake, make a rope of icing with a number five star tube right round the edge of the cake. While the rope is still wet, carefully lift the loosened run-out from the waxed paper and place in position with the pattern exactly corresponding to the collar round the base of the cake. The collar should be a little raised from the cake, and not flat on the iced surface.

Sometimes a silver braid is put round the top of the cake before putting on the rope of icing to hold the collar. This neatens the edge and is a support for the collar.

Completing the cake

Add any final decorations—swans, ballet dancers, animals, etc., and prop in position with tissue-paper until the icing fixing them to the cake surface is quite firm and dry (pls. *125*, *126* and *134*). A fine silver braid can be used to tidy the cake between the base and the run-out sugar, especially if the white icing is tinged from a coloured run-out. If preferred pipe small scrolls or stars.

If the student is unfortunate enough to break the collar in two or three places, it can be pieced together with a little icing. When quite dry, these joins can be disguised with a piped flower or fern. This will not pass in examination work, but it can still look attractive for home purposes.

Smaller sections of run-out work

A large run-out design can be cut into small sections, made as individual pieces and assembled on the cake top to form a complete run-out design. Rectangular pieces can be placed alternately with lacy patterns or flowers (pl. *127*). This looks particularly effective, and the pieces are far easier to handle, and easier to replace if a breakage does occur. Fasten with a small dot of icing.

CHAPTER SIXTEEN

The Combination of Lace Work and Run-out Work

There is something doubly fascinating when these two forms of sugarcraft are used in the same piece of work. It is essential to design the basic shape of the pattern with some solid and some lacy work before beginning the actual icing. The lace work need not be the same pattern throughout. Even on one small section of the design, the lace pattern can be varied. This is what makes the combination of lace and run-out work so dainty and exciting.

Prepare this work in the usual way, fixing the greaseproof paper pattern onto a sheet of glass and covering with waxed paper. Firstly, outline the design, secondly fill in the lace work, and finally run in the soft sugar work, using a fine paint brush or a bag, as a teaspoon may hold too much and overflow the icing onto the lace work. As a guide, *see* plate *129*, showing the preparation of lace and run-out work for a wedding cake. See also pl. *174* for similar work finished.

A SQUARE CAKE WITH ROSES
(pl. *128*)

The cake in this particular photograph has four sections of lace and run-out work, one along each side of the cake. Begin in the usual way by drawing the pattern on greaseproof, copying the design from the picture. Fasten down on a sheet of glass and cover with thin waxed paper. Make each section on a separate piece of waxed paper, or there will be a danger of breakage when the pieces of icing are removed. Make several extra sections so that no time is wasted while replacements dry.

Using a number one tube, outline the pattern, and then make the lace work, filling in with the letter "*x*" in the centre,

and loops in the side. Finally, run-in the soft sugar icing, completing each section before beginning work on the next.

While these sections are drying, make sure that the cake and board are completed. The surface of the cake should be perfectly finished, and the board should be four inches wider on all sides than the actual cake. Cut out the main outlines of the pattern and trace onto the board. Work similarly to the top sections, and fill in the soft sugar work close up to the edge of the cake and round the edge of the design. When dry, outline with a fine tube and add several dots to give a finish to the centre of the soft sugar edging (pl. *128*).

While the board work is drying, pipe some bells on a well-greased metal bell mould, and when dry, remove by holding in front of the fire and easing off very carefully as the grease melts. Place on cotton wadding until needed. Tie four strips of silver ribbon into four bows and place at the lower corners held in place with stiff icing. Fix the bells near the ribbon, two at each corner, resting on the board, again using icing to secure in place.

To fix the top lace sections

Although these lace pieces have wide run-out work on the inside edges to attach them to the cake, it is still necessary to hold them in position until quite dry. Pile some books or a similar substitute, to the correct height of the corners of the cake, and on top of the pile place a ruler against the edge of the cake. This supports the lace work until it is set firmly in place. Run a line of icing along the edge of the cake, and after removing the waxed paper, place one of the lace work sections in place and at the same time, set the opposite section in place. Leave the cake un-

142. *Top left*—Plain circular run-outs and small sugar-centred daisies employ an unusual colour scheme: white and yellow.

143. *Top right*—A square cake with two unusual features: a three-tiered run-out and a use of mirrors under each half bell and under the central scene as a lake.

144. *Centre left*—Lace and run-out decorate the Christmas design of a run-out candle with an inset picture, red poinsettia flowers and piped green tinted leaves.

145. *Bottom right*—A realistic picture in 3-D run-out icing, the sky and star painted and piped straight on to the cake, and the boy and donkey are made on a forward layer of icing. Note the neat rope rows of icing holding up the top collar and the band of silver braid to neaten on the outside.

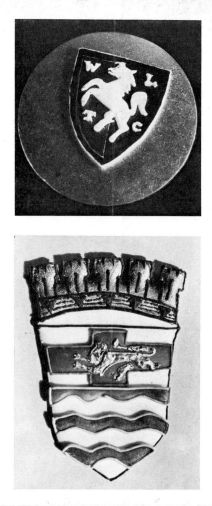

146. *Top left*—A sea scene in 3-D, the sky and clouds painted on to the cake, sea and ships added next, jetty and boat-house in the foreground. Note the tiny loops hanging on the run-out edge.

147. *Top right*—A school badge run-out from a tracing taken from a blazer.

148. *Centre left*—The coats of arms of London and Australia, a lifebelt, Tower Bridge, the Forth Bridge and Sydney Bridge crown a splendidly elaborate design for a family emigrating.

149. *Centre right*—The coat of arms of the London County Council made for a council tea, each section run-out separately and mounted on the background.

150. *Bottom right*—A cake to mark the royal opening of a new church: mounted on the top tier is the bishop's personal crest. Lace work angels edge the cake.

151. *Top left*—A thatched cottage cake, green icing used for grass and a mirror to represent a pond.

152. *Centre left*—Model church made in pastillage sections joined and windows made with royal icing, bricks marked with a knife; vary the green coconut grass surround with an icing path sprinkled with sago or sugar.

153. *Bottom left*—Flowers over the door give an individual touch to a cottage cake covered mainly in almond paste.

154. *Bottom right*—An oblong, loaf-shaped cake is formed into a windmill. The sails are made from icing piped on to wire.

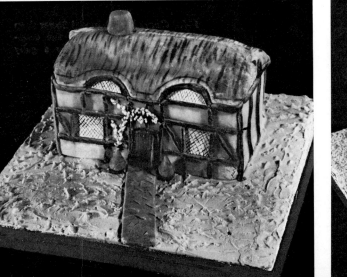

155. *Top left*—Roughed green icing 'grass' surrounds this cottage which is thatched with strands of a breakfast cereal.

156. *Top right*—Kentish oast houses made from two swiss rolls cut to shape and covered with almond paste and moulded gum paste.

157. *Centre left*—A model flower shop with piped flowers behind the cellophane window, sheltered by a gaily coloured piped sunblind.

158. *Bottom left*—The village smithy with a piped thatched roof and a cobblestone surround made from balls of cold fondant pressed flat on to lightly iced board.

159. Top right—
The ideal model birthday cake for a boy; basis is swiss roll and madeira cakes covered with cold fondant; wheels, engine front and cabin are all made in run-out icing and the cabin is filled with liquorice 'coal'.

160. Centre—A cake banjo covered with marzipan and iced with piping 'strings'.

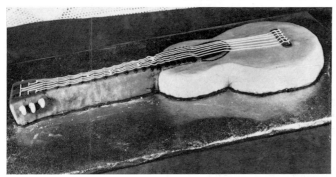

162. Bottom right—
Unusual decoration for a wedding cake is made from a wire circle covered with foil and decorated with bells, silver leaves and small flowers.

161. Bottom left—A cake model of Bodiam Castle, the sections covered with gum paste and marked with a knife to represent stone-work; gardens with birds and flowers, and a moat with swans and water-lilies are all represented and the model can be floodlit by wiring up a small electric light bulb placed inside the walls.

163. *Top left*—Three tiers of a wedding cake ready to be assembled, each showing identical designs, graduated in size. The scalloped design on the cake sides is piped with a fine star tube, with the aid of a template.

164. *Centre left*—A wedding cake designed so simply that it could be carried out by a first year student.

166. *Bottom right*—A simply designed wedding cake using the eight point star design and gum paste roses.

165. *Centre right*—An unusual wedding cake designed to incorporate butterflies and medallions taken from the wedding dress lace material.

167. *Top left*—A simple three tier cake using bought ornaments and topped with the brides' christening cup.

168. *Top right*—A design with a little more intricacy, but as the ornaments are all bought, this should still be well within the scope of a comparatively new student.

169. *Bottom left*—A nursing and a college badge illustrate the careers of bride and groom on the bottom tier of a neat, simple cake.

170. *Bottom right*— Loops fastened on stars to hang away from the cake sides provide an elaborate finish to an elaborate cake.

171. *Top left.* A harvest time wedding cake using the traditional wedding ornamentation of bunches of grapes, designed in a pattern to follow through to the base of the cake and to the cake board

172. *Top right*— Thistles decorate an unusually shaped wedding cake.

173. *Bottom left*— Run-out corner pieces and heart shapes edged with a frill of icing from a petal tube, decorate this three tier cake.

174. *Bottom right*— Lace and run-out work combine to make a neat design, incorporating the bride and groom's initials and delicate run-out flowers.

disturbed with both sections set in place in a warm room for two or three days until completely dry. Draw the books away carefully, one at a time, perhaps removing one jutting out from the pile first. Very great care must be taken, as the least vibration will shake the lace work and break it. Repeat exactly the same procedure to fix the remaining two lace sections in place.

To complete the cake

Make four birds and place one at each top corner, centering the cake with three large gum tragacanth or pastillage roses and a few silver leaves. This design is suitable for a three-tier wedding cake—one will be seen later in this book—or perhaps for a 21st birthday cake, with a suitable inscription and lace work "21", standing in the centre. It is not generally satisfactory for transporting any great distance, although if this is absolutely necessary, settle the cake on the floor of a car on several cushions to take any vibration, and it can be safely and carefully taken on a short journey.

DOUBLE RUN-OUTS
(pls. *134, 135* and *136*)

This method is a combination of large, plain run-out and lace. Complete the large run-out first on waxed paper, and the reflection round the cake on the board. Make lace or lace and soft sugar pieces to follow the outer line of the plain run-out shape. Plan similar pieces, or simply plain run-outs for the board. Fix the pieces in position with hidden stars of icing. Before fixing any of the top run-outs in place, complete any other decorations or writing to avoid the slightest chance of breaking the fragile lace work.

THE "WELCOME" CAKE
(pl. *130*)

The first layer of plain run-out placed on the cake has four cut-out semicircles,

filled in with trellis on the back. The plain sections which have not been cut-out are then topped with a second piece of run-out and lace work, following exactly the same basic design, and centred with a lacy pattern. In this particular photograph, the letters of *welcome* have been outlined in pale-pink sugar and then run-in straight onto the good surface of the cake, using pale-pink soft sugar icing, but these can also be made in advance on waxed paper, and then placed in position (pls. *139* and *140*). This method is preferable for dark coloured letters, as they may run into the white icing if outlined and run-in straight onto the cake surface.

A spray of anemones and a sprig of fern complete this cake.

COMPLETE DOUBLE RUN-OUTS
(pl. *131*)

This particular photograph shows a wedding cake using whole double run-outs. A plain shaped run-out is placed on the cake first, and then covered with a lacy section exactly the same shape and size as the original run-out, with a large bell let into the work. A star fixes the two run-outs, raising the top one a little from the first plain one underneath. The edges are joined with a loop pattern. The monogram of the initials "A" and "M" was run-out on waxed paper first, and placed on the cake, again using a slight "raising" star.

A template should be cut to make the dainty hanging loop design on the side of the cake. This must always be completed before putting the main run-outs in place.

RUN-OUTS RAISED FROM
THE BOARD

Sometimes it is useful to be able to raise the bottom run-out next to the board by half an inch or so, as in plate **37**. For this, the run-out should be made on waxed

G

paper as before, but the diameter of the centre circle should be half an inch larger, as the whole run-out has to be placed over the cake, before it can be fixed in position. Place several large stars on the board, about half an inch from the side of the cake, and leave to set. These will support the run-out circle. When dry, place second stars alternately between the first stars, and while still wet, lower the dry run-out circle very carefully over the cake and into position. Make sure it is level, and then leave to set firmly in place. Neaten by filling in the quarter inch space between cake and circle with a row of icing stars or beads.

For further ideas and designs study the photographs of cakes combining lace and run-out work in plates *133*, *137*, *141*, *144* and *173*.

CHAPTER SEVENTEEN

Three Dimensional Run-outs and Heraldry

The art of three dimensional work is one of the most fascinating forms of cake decorating. An artist can draw freehand pictures from fact or imagination: a local road; a holiday place; a building or a particular house. For those who are not gifted artistically, a picture from a magazine, Christmas or birthday card will serve as well as a freehand drawing.

Begin by studying the card or picture. The background—sky, clouds, and perhaps a few trees—can be painted onto the cake in edible colour. Next, cut three circles or squares of greaseproof paper the size and shape of the top of the cake.

On one piece of paper trace a horizon or sky-line in the background consisting of hills, houses or perhaps another tree. Make sure to take this line to the edge of the paper.

On a second piece of paper trace a line in the foreground perhaps using the line of a bridge or fencing, again extending the line to the edge of the paper where necessary.

On the third paper trace any figures in the immediate foreground and bring the line again to the edge of the paper as the figure must have ground to stand on and not appear in mid-air. A study of the coloured photograph showing the run-out sections will demonstrate how the work is planned.

Place these three papers on top of one another and study the balance of the picture before beginning the icing. It may be necessary to add another tree or figure. Sometimes sections from a second Christmas card can be used with the first to improve the proportions of a picture.

Place each sheet of paper on glass and fasten down with a few dots of icing near the top so that they are not under the run-out. Cover with waxed paper and fasten down again. With a number one tube and white royal icing outline the tracing line in the first pattern—the skyline of hills and houses and right round the lower edge to make a continuous line. Flood with soft sugar. In the same way outline the traced foreground line of the second picture, continuing round the lower edge of the paper. Again flood with soft sugar. Finally outline the figures and the edge of the last pattern, and flood to make a third run-out. The result will be rather unusual in appearance, but when completed the picture soon takes shape.

Keep these pieces in a warm place for two or three days and when quite dry outline the original tracing on the back of the greaseproof with a soft pencil and re-trace the appropriate sections of the picture onto the dry iced cake and onto the pieces of run-out, using a sharp pencil but pressing only lightly to avoid breaking the run-out. A thin outline will be left on the icing as a guide. Using a fine artist's brush paint in the picture with edible colour diluted with water, allowing only a very little dampness on the brush or the sugar will dissolve and the icing become sticky. When colouring all these sections it is only necessary to paint about half an inch below where the next section will come and not to the lowest edge of the cake (pl. **40**). Emphasize any thick parts —fir trees, tops of houses, rough pieces of snow on the trees and ground—with fine lines of piping and coloured icing. Figures of people and tree trunks can be outlined and flooded lightly to give a rounded effect.

When all the sections have been completed and are quite dry, they must be put together. Using white icing and a star tube, make a rope of icing all round the top edge of the cake, and one or two stars in the centre to prop up the run-out sections. Place the first section in position, and then make a second rope of icing right round the cake. Try to keep this rope "wall" neat, as although it can often be tidied with silver braid, it may show on some cakes (pl. *145*). Carefully lower the second section into position, if necessary allowing the icing rope and stars to dry a little first, and perhaps adding more stars to fix the run-out in place.

Secure all the run-out sections and complete the board with a run-out surface to match the top collar. Have ready the run-out top collar, either plain or with lace insets and an edging of picot dots. Place this in position last of all, fastened with a final ring of icing. Plate **41** shows a completed cake with all the sections shown in plate **40** fixed in position.

These elaborate cakes are not usually saleable commercially, but they are interesting to build up, fascinating to compose, and they almost always result in orders from friends for special occasion cakes. For further examples of three dimensional run-outs, *see* plates **42** to **45**.

HERALDRY

A school badge or shield (plate *147*) is simple to represent, and makes one of the appropriate decorations for a schoolboy's birthday party cake or for a big school function. Coats-of-arms, family crests and national emblems are all equally easy to work, although strict attention must be paid to correct details (plates *148* to *150*).

Before beginning the work, take a tracing of the badge from a blazer pocket, using greaseproof paper and a soft pencil. Improve on the drawing with a little freehand touching up. If there is no emblem of the correct size available, copy a picture from a school magazine or note-paper heading. Also make separate tracings of the different sections of the crest.

When the tracings are completed, fasten down on a sheet of glass and cover with a thin layer of waxed paper. Begin the icing work by outlining the outer edge of the tracing of the entire crest, and fill with run-out icing of the palest colour. Outline the other sections, and fill these with the appropriate colours. When all the pieces are dry, fix together, holding in position with a little icing underneath.

Touch in any extra details with edible colour and a paint brush, mixing gold powder with a little gin or any other spirit for use as gilding. Used in small quantities, this is perfectly safe to eat, although it is generally meant only for decoration. Final lines can be added and emphasized by over-piping with a double-nought tube.

Finish the badge on one side only if it is to lie flat on the cake surface, otherwise it must be completed perfectly on both sides and stood upright (pl. *150*), so that it is attractive from any angle.

27. *Top right*—A Santa Claus run-out with colouring in progress.

28. *Bottom right*—A variety of methods of cake decoration in one cake: run-out figures and mistletoe, trees half run-out and half lace work piping, and lanterns made from gum paste and lace piping.

29. *Bottom left*—Christmas cake decorated with run-outs, the main decoration worked on both sides, the side decoration worked on to the curved baking tin covered with waxed paper.

30. *Top left*—A child's birthday "merry-go-round" cake covered in cold fondant and edged with horses run-out on both sides. Bonus birthday present: modelled black dog and shopping basket.

31. *Centre right*—21st birthday cake decorated with a lily pond of run-out swans and a large run-out key.

32. *Centre left*—Christmas cake decorated with a large Santa Claus, run-out on both sides, the run-out of the child in bed worked on waxed paper on the side of the cake tin. The cake is neatened with plain circular run-outs on cake and board.

33. *Bottom right*—Gay Christmas cake, the central figures run-out on both sides and surrounded with an unusually shaped collar.

34. *Top left*—Four cakes with run-out collars and figures, made especially for children. The two lower cakes illustrate nursery stories, the two upper cakes show a park scene and three cats playing.

35. *Top right*—A brilliantly coloured icing stained-glass window decorates an unusual Christmas cake.

36. *Centre left*—Christmas cake decorated with run-out collar and figures.

37. *Bottom right*—Raised run-outs decorate this Christmas cake to allow room for the icicles to hang, roughened icing snow edges the run-out, the run-out figures are worked on both sides, and rock sugar is used to make piles of snow.

38. *Top left*—Semi-circular run-outs joined with lace work give a round cake a square effect; raised icing has been used to make the picture on the centre and sides of the cake stand out.

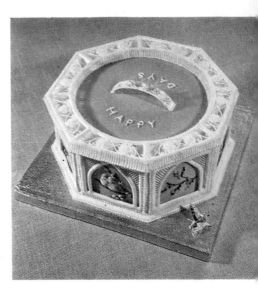

39. *Top right*—A dainty summertime cake made in the shape of a casket with a lacy handle.

40. *Centre left*—Run-out sections prepared to build up the 3–d design shown in pl. **41.** The largest piece is put first on to the previously painted cake surface, then the bridge section is added, and lastly the snowman and trees.

41. *Bottom right*—The completed 3–d run-out picture using the sections shown in pl. **40.**

43. *Centre left*—A deep 3–d design with layers of snow-covered land built up one by one and a river painted straight on to the cake.

42. *Top right*—A 3–d Swiss scene framed by an unusually shaped outer collar.

44. *Bottom right*—A wintry scene taken from a Christmas card using the 3–d sections as in pl. **40.**

45. *Top left*—Carol singers at a church doorway, the inside of the church painted on to the cake surface, the archway brought forward, and the figures placed in position in the foreground.

46. *Top right*—A cake incorporating the badge of a women's institute, the colours carried through the design outline and the corner roses.

47. *Centre right*—A small model country cottage with piped icing cabbages in the vegetable garden.

48. *Bottom left*—A model village made entirely in cake and icing, down to the vintage car, the lake and gardens; see plates *151* to *158* for details.

49. *Top left*—And for a girl, a Wendy House modelled from two fruit cakes placed one on top of the other and covered with cold fondant.

50. *Top right*—A model of the Christmas crib, filled with gum paste figures fixed in position with icing stars and propped until dry.

51. *Centre right*—A book cake with a page copied from a child's nursery book makes a suitable cake for a party. Learn from the mistake in this photograph and work out wording and lettering on paper before beginning to work on the actual cake.

52. *Bottom left*—A crinoline lady for an unusual birthday cake: the basis is a madeira or fruit cake, baked in a basin and covered with almond paste or cold fondant and a layer of royal icing; the dress is piped, using a petal tube to form the flounces. The china head is placed in position after the skirt is completed.

53. *Top left*—Blue Wedgwood wedding cake.

54/55. *Bottom*—Exhibition and medal winning cakes made by Mr. C. G. Brown of Eltham.

CHAPTER EIGHTEEN

Making and Designing Cake Models

A cake modelled to represent a specific house or church always provokes delight and admiration. It is interesting to work, and a very personal gift to receive. Model cakes can be made to represent almost anything: a particular house or garden, an imaginary model, or a picture building. In the photographs used to illustrate this chapter (pls. *151–158*), students of one class made up a model village for an exhibition (pl. **48**). Their models indicate some of the variety which can be achieved: church, houses, windmill, smithy and gardens (pls. *151–158*).

MAKING A CAKE MODEL

Use a Madeira or fruit cake mixture, and bake in a square or oblong tin, depending on the shape of the model, the occasion, and the amount of work to be put onto the cake. Avoid hollowing the centre of the cake mixture before baking, but tend rather to produce a cake which has risen to a point. If the cake does not rise, a piece will have to be cut from the side to build up the top into a roof using jam to fix the pieces into position and a piece of almond paste to fill in the spaces between the cake sections.

Aim at a well-shaped roof on a model house or shop although a church (pl. *152*) or other complicated models may have to be made in two or three pieces and put together after part decoration (pl. *159*).

The covering

A variety of mixtures can be used to cover the outside of model cakes—almond paste, cold fondant, run-out icing pieces, or even gum paste tragacanth, which gives a good appearance and, although rather hard for general use, is readily eaten by children at a party.

Royal icing can be used for piping structural decorations, and flowers and trees in the garden. Pressed maidenhair and asparagus fern can be used for trees with icing trunks, and green coconut can be spread on royal icing to represent grass. Use coloured sugar for paths and soil, and brown sugar for sand. If necessary, pieces of rustless wire covered with icing may be used to give strength to trees, bridges, gateways and arches.

Beginning the model

Make sure that the cake is on a board large enough to hold the planned garden. Measure the cake carefully and make a paper pattern the exact size of the outside of the house. Lay the pattern on rolled out cold fondant or almond paste, and cut out the pieces with a sharp knife. Scissors will also be useful for trimming. Coat the paste thinly with apricot jam and place on the cake, arranging the pieces neatly, pressing well into position and making neat joins at the corners of walls and roofs. Leave to dry.

Meanwhile cover the roof with a layer of almond paste, like the walls, especially if it has been built up from pieces of cake, and then cut circles of coloured paste which can be arranged overlapping, beginning at the lower edge, like the Wendy house in plate **49**. Arrange a paste chimney, and model any pieces needed for the garden—steps, figures—or for the house—doors and shutters for the windows. Alternatively, run-out pieces of icing can be made the correct size to represent the walls of the house, and fixed on the cake with royal icing. Gum paste or pastillage also makes a good roof as it holds its shape well (pl. *152*).

Piping the details

Using a well-beaten royal icing, pipe in windows, doors, strands of straw for a thatched roof, crazy paving and so on. Often a picture is useful at this stage. Spread the board with thin royal icing, bringing it right up to the model. Sprinkle with green coconut to represent grass. Pipe in flower beds, filling them with dark-brown sugar soil. Place flowers, piped beforehand, into position in the garden.

Animals, motor cars and people can be modelled in cold fondant and fixed in position with a bulb of icing. Prop until dry and firm. Let the imagination run riot in building up these models—the more detail, the greater the children's delight. If possible, let older children help to make them, developing their sense of achievement and creative self-expression.

FLAT MODELS (pl. *160*)

Decide on the shape of the model, and then make a paper pattern. Musical instruments—violin, banjo, double bass— are easy to model and good for a musical party. Bake a Madeira cake in a large, flat meat roasting tin. If the model is large, two cakes may be needed. Using the paper pattern, cut the cake to shape, fixing any joins together with apricot jam.

Roll out a quantity of almond paste, cut to shape, coat with jam and lay on the cake. Place on a long silver board and pipe in strings, pegs, and any other details, making sure first that these details are correct (pl. *160*).

MODELLING FIGURES

Perhaps the best media for modelling are cold fondant and marzipan with a little extra icing sugar added. Storks, cradles, and other white ornaments for christening and wedding cakes can be made from pastillage, but generally this is not the best material to use as it hardens too quickly, and any modelling has to be carried out simply and accurately at speed.

Some people are born with a natural gift for modelling figures. Even so, this is something that anyone, with patience, can learn to do. Try first to make the bodies of the figures in the right proportion. Then, choosing the most suitable tools to hand—knife, skewer, pin, etc.— put in the details. Taking care and time, realistic, exciting results can come simply from studying a picture or, better still, a real life subject.

CHAPTER NINETEEN

Wedding and Special Occasion Cakes

On birthdays, at Christmas and Easter time, when a young couple announce their engagement—these are all the times when the cake decorator and the unusual and decorative cake come into their own. But chief among all these special occasion cakes is the cake that is made for a wedding.

PREPARATION
FOR A WEDDING CAKE

Choosing the right tin

Use square, round, heart-shaped or horseshoe-shaped tins, varying each tier in size, taking, as a rough guide, three round tins ten, eight and six inches, eleven, nine and seven inches, or even twelve, nine and six inches in diameter. However, it is most usual to have a difference of two inches between each tier.

Line the tin with double greaseproof paper and tie a double fold of brown paper round the outside. Place on a baking-sheet with a layer of salt, sand or cardboard underneath to save direct heat contacting the cake. Make sure that the baking-sheet is not tight to the sides of the oven as the heat must be able to circulate freely round the cake. Horseshoe and number shaped cakes often have no base, in which case it is advisable to place the tin on two baking-sheets if possible.

Placing correctly in the oven

Always use the centre of the oven, and never bake more than one cake at a time unless the centre shelf is large enough to take the two tins at once. Some domestic ovens are not deep enough to take a cake with a diameter of twelve inches. In this case, a ten-inch cake will have to be substituted for the bottom tier, with upper tiers of eight and six inches, or seven and four inches.

Calculating correct quantities

The following recipe is sufficient for an eight-inch round tin, making a cake three inches deep. For a ten-inch tin, use one and a half times the quantities given. For a six-inch tin, use half the quantities. For a square cake, use one and a quarter times each quantity.

As the higher tiers of a wedding cake become smaller, so the depth should decrease correspondingly. This gives good proportion to the cake, which otherwise would look top-heavy. If, after baking, the cake is still not the correct depth, cut down, or build up with marzipan, to produce the correct balance. Level the top of a cake that has risen in the centre, or if the depth of the cake will not allow for cutting, build up the edges with extra almond paste, until the surface is flat. The top of a wedding cake must always be perfectly flat.

Baking time

The baking time given in this recipe is correct for a middle sized cake. Bake one hour more for the largest, and one hour less for the smallest. The temperature is the same for all sizes.

RECIPE FOR A WEDDING CAKE

8 ozs. butter.
8 ozs. dark brown sugar.
10 oz. plain flour.
4 eggs (large).
2 ozs. ground almonds.
Pinch salt.

1 level teaspoon mixed spice.
1 teaspoon instant coffee.
1 teaspoon cocoa.
8 ozs. currants.
8 ozs. blue raisins (small).
8 ozs. Valencia raisins (stoned).
8 ozs. sultanas.
2 ozs. cherries.
2 ozs. candied peel.
1 dessertspoon dark treacle.
   Grated rind of 1 orange and 1 lemon.

Method: Wash and dry all fruit the day before mixing the cake. Have the eight-inch round tin prepared, lined with two sheets of greaseproof paper and with double brown paper tied round the outside.

Cream the butter and sugar until very light. Add eggs, one at a time, one teaspoon-ful of flour, salt, treacle, spices, orange and lemon rind. Mix well. Fold in the flour, adding the fruit and peel, and the cherries which should have been rolled in flour. Mix thoroughly and put into the lined tin. Heat a gas oven for ten minutes beforehand to a No. 1 regulo, or an electric oven for twenty minutes to a heat of 250° to 275°F., so that the heat is steady. Place the cake in the centre of the oven and cook for four and a half to six hours. This long, slow cooking gives a good, rich, dark colour.

When cooked, allow to cool in the tin for about ten minutes, and then turn out onto a wire tray. When cold, wrap in greaseproof paper and put into a tin. If there is no suitable tin, wrap in foil. Keep for about three or four weeks before icing. When the cake is about a week old, prick the top in several places with a skewer and pour a little spirits over the cake from a teaspoon. Make sure there is not too much spirit to be absorbed into the small holes, as the cake should not be made wet. Wrap up again afterwards in the greaseproof paper and foil.

Almond paste

These quantities are very variable. The amount of almond paste depends on how much it is liked, and how much money is to be spent, as almonds are expensive. To make enough paste for a good half-inch covering all over an eight-inch cake, use:

1 lb. ground almonds.
1 lb. castor sugar.
1 lb. icing sugar.
2 to 3 eggs or 4 yolks if the whites are required for royal icing.
A little spirits, lemon juice or orange flower water.

Follow the method described in Chapter Two. These quantities will cover a similar sized square cake, although the covering will be a little thinner. The least amount of paste that can possibly be used for a satisfactory result, is half these quantities.

COVERING WITH ROYAL ICING

Make up about one pound of icing sugar to coat the cake. It is impossible to make exactly the right amount of icing, with none left over, as there must be sufficient to cover the cake and then to scrape off smoothly leaving a good surface.

Following the methods described in Chapter Three, begin by icing the largest cake first, making sure to wipe the silver board clean after each layer of icing is completed. Avoid putting on the icing too thickly and allow each surface to dry thoroughly in a warm room for two or three days—an airing cupboard is useful for the first two or three hours. At least three or four coats of icing will be necessary, but the finished thickness must not be more than a quarter of an inch. Use sandpaper between each coat to remove any roughness.

In between coats, icing can be kept under a damp cloth or in an airtight container until it is used again, although before beating, the icing must be transferred from the container to a porcelain bowl. Make up the icing as needed using albumen and another pound of icing sugar, and beating in the left over icing when the new icing is ready. Three to four pounds of icing sugar should be

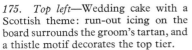

175. *Top left*—Wedding cake with a Scottish theme: run-out icing on the board surrounds the groom's tartan, and a thistle motif decorates the top tier.

176. *Top right*—American style wedding cake, the three tiers placed directly on top of one another with no pillars in between.

177. *Bottom left*—A bought decoration stands at the top of this very ornamental heart-shaped wedding cake.

178. *Centre right*—Lace and run-out work standing over the edge of the cake decorate this dainty wedding cake.

179. *Bottom right*—Run-outs decorate this two tier cake on a mirror base. The horseshoe ornament is also run-out work.

180. *Top left*—White holly leaves and golden berries decorate a wintertime golden wedding cake; the trellis '50' stands on plaques with the names John and Mary.

181. *Top right*—The top tier of a wedding cake has been saved and turned into a christening cake by adding a run-out cradle with a gum paste coverlet, standing on a gum paste plaque. Also shown is an alternative design for a cradle, and a plaque with the baby's initials.

182. *Centre left*—A cake suitable for a tea party after a confirmation; the prayer book covers are run-out pieces, gilded with gilt powder mixed with spirits.

183. *Bottom left*—A 21st birthday cake for someone keen on dancing and music; the drums and keys are modelled from pastillage.

184. *Bottom right*—To make this wintery cake, a plain run-out collar is covered with royal icing pulled up roughly with the back of a knife, while reindeer complete the snowy scene on the cake surface.

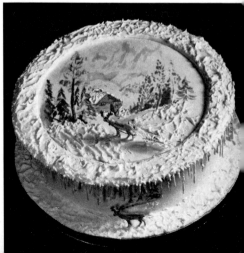

185. *Top left*—Valentine cakes decorated with freehand piped hyacinths and lettering, run-out work used only for the flower vases and heart-shaped flowers.

186. *Centre left*—An unusual Easter cake, the yellow catkins made first on waxed paper with dots of royal icing clustered on top of each other, the birds run-out and the nest and branches piped in chocolate.

187. *Centre right*—Fluffy yellow Easter chick decorates a gay springtime cake.

188. *Bottom left*—A cuckoo clock cake, the blue birds and piped flowers all made previously on waxed paper and then placed in position.

189. *Bottom right*—Two Easter cakes decorated with pussy willow catkins and neatened with plain run-out collars.

190. *Top left*—Run-out choir-boys and lettering are raised slightly on small stars of icing to decorate this Christmas cake.

191. *Top right*—Exhibition cake by Mr C. G. Brown representing a casket.

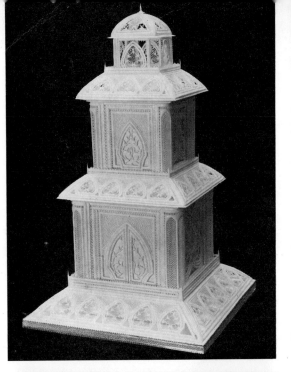

192. *Above*—A 21st birthday cake which could be adapted for a twin's birthday or for an engagement.

Exhibition cakes by Mr. C. G. Brown

193. *Above*—a very neat run-out top to this cake with built up circles. Note—side treatment of the cake and work on the board.

195. *Below*—Single tier wedding cake with built up circular edge.

194. *Bottom left*—A novelty retirement cake which tells its own story.

sufficient to complete a three-tiered wedding cake, although this inevitably depends on the thickness of the covering and the number of coats needed for a good result. The final coat should be very thin, just enough to give a good finish to the sandpapered surface.

Stiffen any left over icing by beating well, only adding more sugar or albumen to bring up to piping strength for working the design. The boards on which the wedding cakes stand must always be whitened with a thin coat of icing and decorated with braiding, trellis or lacework—study the photographs for ideas.

SUITABLE DESIGNS FOR A WEDDING CAKE

For general ideas, refer to the photographs used in this book to illustrate wedding cakes (pls. *162–179*), and also to Chapter Seven for template designs. A wide range of ornaments can be bought for the top of a wedding cake—silver vases with natural flowers to match the bride's bouquet, or perhaps a modelled sugar ornament. A useful idea is to buy a stiff metal bracelet for about threepence, or to bend a piece of wire into a similar round shape, covering it neatly with silver foil. Using stiff icing, attach silver leaves, bought lily of the valley and piped sugar roses to the silver circle, and stand upright on the top of the cake on a gum paste plaque, fixed in position with a star of icing (pl. *162*). Prop with tissue-paper until dry.

Round or square pillars can be bought from two to four inches high (pl. *163*). The middle three-inch size is usually the best. If the cake is large, it is advisable to cover the bottom tier with a thin silver board to take the weight of the two tiers above (pl. *166*). If the icing is sufficiently dry, this should not be necessary in a two-tier cake.

THE STAND

Arrangements for hiring a cake stand should be made weeks in advance of the wedding. Contact a local confectioner, who will usually be able to hire out a good cake knife as well, and perhaps even a silver vase.

CUTTING THE CAKE

When the cake has been ceremonially cut by the bride and bridegroom, it should be taken from the reception room to complete the cutting. Begin by cutting straight across the centre, and then into strips one inch wide across the cake. Lay these pieces flat on a board and cut into fingers. Some icing will always fall away from the cake as it is cut, but this method is far more satisfactory than trying to cut wedge-shaped pieces, which always causes the icing to crumble at the centre of the cake.

Place any loose icing neatly on top of the cake pieces, and arrange on plates to be handed round, and in boxes to be sent away.

DESIGNING TO MATCH A DRESS
(pl. *165*)

An attractively personal wedding cake can be made by incorporating the actual lace used for the wedding dress or veil of the bride into the design on the cake. Keep a few scraps of the material, particularly lace edging, and carefully cut out medallions and butterflies, cutting each wing separately. Cut some half medallion shapes for the base of the cake, and place all the lace pieces on waxed paper. Pipe round the edges, and perhaps into the pattern as well. Pipe the centre of the butterfly wings, and leave to dry thoroughly.

Meanwhile, for the cake in the photograph, arrange silver braid round the cake in two places, dividing the depth of the cake into thirds. Just overlap the silver braids with a satin ribbon right round the centre of the cake. Pipe stars round the top edge and make hanging loops suspended from them. When these are quite dry, turn the cake upside down and make

H

corresponding loops from the base of the cake.

Make the trellis work for the corners round a wooden spoon handle, or anything else suitably shaped, greased and covered with double wax-paper. Pipe rings for the centre pieces, strengthening with fine wire. When these are dry, decorate with small piped roses and leaves—pale pink and green leaves for a birthday cake, but all white for a wedding cake.

When all the preparation is complete, begin to assemble the cake. Fix the trellis pieces in position with piped shells of royal icing. Place the half medallions on the board, and the full medallions correspondingly round the top of the cake, slightly jutting over the edge. Make a body for the

butterflies either straight onto the cake, or previously on waxed paper, sticking the wings into the wet icing and propping with tissue-paper until firm. If the entire butterfly is made first onto waxed paper, fix to the cake with a small dab of icing.

Lastly, arrange the rings of roses, securing with a dab of icing on the side nearest the outside of the cake, and propping up on the inside with tissue-paper until dry. If the cake is to be a two-tier wedding cake, complete a similar cake in a smaller size, and place the pillars to hold this second cake inside the rose rings.

To adapt this design for a 21st birthday, make the figure "21" in trellis, and stand in the centre of the rose rings.

CHAPTER TWENTY

Recipes

Before baking a cake for any special occasion, get to know the oven. Ovens vary in temperature, and thermostats and thermometers are not always correct. Make a mental note of best and worst results, and learn by experience.

VICTORIA SANDWICH

Ingredients:
4 ozs. margarine or butter.
4 ozs. castor sugar.
4 ozs. self-raising flour (or plain flour and 1 level teaspoon baking powder).
2 large eggs.

Method: Heat the oven to No. **3 or 4** regulo, or 275° to 325°F., in an electric oven, and grease two seven-inch or one eight-inch tin, lining the base with a round of paper. Cream the margarine and sugar until very light. Add one egg and a teaspoonful of flour and beat well. Add the second egg and another teaspoonful of flour and continue beating. Sift in the remaining flour through a good, large sieve, and fold in lightly. If small eggs have been used, fold in two teaspoons of milk or warm water. Bake for forty minutes, if all in one tin, or fifteen to twenty minutes if in two tins. When cooked, turn out, cool, and place in a tin until needed. Decorate with glacé icing, butter cream, or fudge or caramel icing.

MADEIRA CAKE

Follow the recipe for a Victoria sandwich, but use 6 ozs. flour. Use as a sandwich cake and decorate with glacé icing or butter cream, fudge or caramel icing. To adapt for the crinoline lady cake, bake in a Pyrex or glass ovenware basin for one and a quarter hours.

PLAIN WHITE CAKE

Ingredients:
8 ozs. self-raising flour (or plain flour and 1 level teaspoon baking powder).
4 ozs. margarine.
½ oz. lard.
4 ozs. castor sugar.
2 eggs (or 1 egg and a little milk).
Vanilla essence.

Method: Rub the margarine and lard into the sifted flour. Add the sugar. Whisk the two eggs until frothy, or if only one egg is used, whisk and then add a little milk. Stir the egg into the flour, etc., beating lightly. Turn into a seven-inch cake tin and bake at No. 3 or 4 regulo (275°–325°F.) for about an hour to an hour and ten minutes.

This cake is suitable for cutting into layers and filling. To vary the layers, use alternately with chocolate cake, or a cake coloured pink with edible colouring or a raspberry blancmange powder mixed with the flour.

To turn this recipe into a plain fruit cake, add four to six ounces of currants or sultanas.

RUSSIAN SANDWICH

Follow the recipe for a plain white cake and divide the mixture into two. Colour half pink. Put spoonfuls of the plain mixture into a greased loaf tin, leaving spaces between the spoonfuls. Brush over with apricot jam. Put spoonfuls of the pink mixture into half the spaces, and colour the remainder with cocoa, adding a little milk and a pinch of baking powder. Fill in the final spaces with this chocolate mixture. Carefully hollow the centre to make the cake rise evenly, but avoid mixing the colours unless a marbled effect is needed.

Bake for an hour to an hour and ten minutes, again at No. 3 or 4 regulo (275°–325°F.).

CHOCOLATE CAKE

Ingredients:

> 8 ozs. self-raising flour (or plain flour and 1 teaspoon baking powder).
> 2 ozs. cocoa.
> 7 ozs. castor sugar.
> 4 ozs. lard.
> 1 egg.
> ¼ pt. milk.
> ½ teaspoon vanilla essence.

Method: Sift the flour and cocoa twice. Rub in the lard. Add the sugar and stir in beaten egg and milk to a soft mixture. Add the vanilla essence. Put teaspoonfuls into round based bun tins and bake at No. 3 or 4 (275°–325°F.) for about twelve minutes or bake in an eight-inch cake tin for about one and a quarter hours at No. 3 regulo (275°F.).

This mixture can be used for a sandwich cake, chocolate mushrooms or chocolate butterfly cakes, or even as a good base for the Italian chocolate torton.

LIGHT FRUIT CAKE

Ingredients:

> 2 eggs.
> 4 ozs. castor sugar.
> 4 ozs. margarine or butter.
> 6 ozs. self-raising flour (or plain flour and ½ teaspoon baking powder).
> 4 to 6 ozs. currants, sultanas or chopped raisins
>   or

> 4 ozs. cherries cut in quarters and rolled in flour
>   or
> 2 ozs. chopped walnuts or a mixture of nuts, cherries and sultanas.
> ½ oz. ground almonds (this is optional, giving the cake a moist consistency).

Method: Cream the margarine and sugar lightly. Add one egg and a teaspoonful of flour. Beat well, and add the second egg and a second teaspoonful of flour. Continue beating until light, but do not allow the mixture to curdle. Fold in the remaining sifted flour, together with the rest of the ingredients.

Turn into a loaf tin about five inches by three inches, a round tin, seven inches in diameter, or a six-inch square tin. Hollow out the centre of the mixture and bake at No. 3 or 4 regulo or 300° to 330°F., for about one hour, until firm to the touch.

CANADIAN FRUIT CAKE

Ingredients:

> 7 ozs. self-raising flour and ¼ teaspoon baking powder (or plain flour and 1 heaped teaspoon baking powder).
> 4 ozs. glacé cherries.
> 1 16-oz. tin well-drained chopped pine-apple.
> 5 ozs. butter or margarine.
> 4½ ozs. castor sugar.
> 2 large eggs.
> 9 ozs. chopped sultanas.
> 3 ozs. chopped candied peel.
> 2 tablespoons brandy or sherry.

Method: Cream the margarine and sugar. Add the eggs one at a time with a tea-spoonful of flour, beating after each addition. Fold in the sifted flour and baking powder, add the fruit, and lastly, the brandy or sherry.

Turn into a seven- or eight-inch tin and bake at No. 3 (300°F.) for one to one and a half hours, until firm and nicely browned. Cover lightly with almond paste and cold fondant.

SPONGE OR ALPINE ROLL

Ingredients:

2 large eggs.
2 ozs. castor sugar.
2 ozs. self-raising flour (or plain flour).
1 tablespoon milk.

Method: Put the eggs and sugar in a basin inside a bowl of hot water. Whisk for about twenty minutes until thick and creamy. When nearly ready, remove from the hot water and continue whisking. Sift the flour and fold in lightly. Fold in the milk. Pour the mixture into a greased and floured swiss roll tin and spread evenly. Bake in the middle of a hot oven, No. 6 regulo, for seven minutes.

While the cake is baking, heat some jam and spread a sheet of greaseproof paper on the table. Dredge the paper well with castor sugar. When the cake is ready, turn out carefully onto the paper, and quickly trim off quarter of an inch all round the edge. Spread with the warm jam and roll up quickly. Hold in position for a few minutes until quite firm and then leave to cool on a wire tray covered with paper or a cloth. To fill the roll with cream instead of jam, roll up with no filling, and when cold, carefully unroll and fill with cream. Used in this way, the recipe will be suitable for making an alpine roll.

Self-raising flour, or plain flour and baking powder, may be used if preferred, but if sufficiently beaten, the mixture should have enough air incorporated to produce a well risen cake without baking powder.

CHOCOLATE ROLL

Ingredients:

2 large eggs.
2 ozs. castor sugar.
2 tablespoons milk.
1 to 2 ozs. cocoa.
1½ ozs. plain flour.

Method: Sift cocoa and flour thoroughly —twice, if necessary—and proceed using the method given for a sponge roll. Bake in the same way, and roll up without jam. When cold, fill with chocolate or white butter cream. This recipe is suitable for making a chocolate log.

SPONGE SANDWICH

Ingredients:

2 large eggs.
2 ozs. castor sugar.
3 ozs. plain flour.
1 tablespoon milk.
Vanilla essence (optional).

Method: Sift the flour, and continue to make up the mixture following the method for mixing a sponge roll. Have ready two sandwich tins six inches across, greased and dredged with flour and sugar. Divide the mixture equally between the two tins. Bake on the middle shelf of the oven, if possible both on the same shelf beside each other, at No. 5 regulo (375°F.), for fifteen to twenty minutes. Cool on a wire tray with a cloth underneath.

Sandwich the cakes together using any of the fillings given earlier in this book. If preferred instead of using two tins, one larger tin can be used, seven or eight inches in diameter, and the cake can be split in half and filled. In this case, bake for twenty-five to thirty minutes.

GENOESE SANDWICH
AND SMALL FANCY CAKES

Ingredients:

3 large eggs.
3 ozs. butter.
4 ozs. castor sugar.
2½ ozs. flour, ½ oz. cornflour (or 3 ozs. flour).

Method: Warm and sift the flour—twice if possible—onto a plate or paper. Whisk the eggs and sugar over hot water, sufficiently to trap enough air to eliminate the need for baking powder. The air alone acts as a raising agent. When the mixture is thick and creamy, fold in the melted butter, and then the flour, lightly but thoroughly. Turn the mixture into two sandwich tins seven inches in diameter, and bake at No. 7 regulo (400°F.) for about twenty minutes.

This mixture may also be baked in an oblong swiss roll tin, and then cut into small pieces to make *petits fours*, domino cakes, or other small fancy cakes. These will keep well, and the mixture is firmer than a sponge cake, and is not so liable to crumble.

SIMNEL CAKE

Ingredients:

Cake mixture—
2 eggs.
5 ozs. margarine or butter.
5 ozs. brown sugar.
7 ozs. self-raising flour (or plain flour and ½ teaspoon baking powder).
6 ozs. sultanas.
2 ozs. currants.
1 oz. candied peel.

Almond paste—
½ lb. ground almonds.
¼ lb. icing sugar.
¼ lb. castor sugar.
1 large egg.
Water or glacé icing, or royal icing.

Method: Cream margarine and brown sugar thoroughly. Add beaten eggs a little at a time with one teaspoonful of flour. Add remaining sifted flour. Stir in fruit and peel. Turn half the mixture into a lined seven-inch tin and cover with a layer of almond paste, using half the amount given in the recipe. Put the remainder of the cake mixture on top of the paste and hollow the centre slightly. Bake at No. 3 (275°F.) until firm to the touch. The skewer method often used to test a cake is not satisfactory, as the almond would only stick to the skewer.

When cold, use the other half of the paste for decoration and to make a bird's nest. Complete with glacé or royal icing,

as described in Chapter Two, and shown in plates *8* and *11*.

CHRISTMAS OR BIRTHDAY CAKE

Ingredients:

½ lb. margarine or butter.
½ lb. dark brown sugar.
4 eggs.
2 lb. mixed fruit.
2 ozs. cherries.
12 to 16 ozs. plain flour.
1 oz. ground almonds.
1 teaspoon mixed spice.
1 tablespoon dark treacle.
Rind of 1 orange and 1 lemon.
2 ozs. candied peel.
A little milk if necessary.

Method: Heat the oven on No. 1, or to 250°F. Line an eight- or nine-inch tin with greaseproof paper and tie some brown paper round the outside of the tin. If possible, clean and dry the fruit the previous day.

Cream the margarine and sugar, add the eggs one at a time with a teaspoonful of flour. Beat after adding each egg. Beat in spice, treacle and grated lemon rind and add the sifted flour, folding in. Add the fruit, almonds, peel, and, if necessary for a good consistency, a little milk.

Turn into the prepared tin and bake for four to six hours. Avoid opening the oven door. This long, slow cooking gives the cake a good, rich, dark colour.

GINGERBREAD PASTRY
(for modelling or for biscuits)

Ingredients:

1 lb. plain flour.
½ teaspoon salt.
1 level tablespoon bicarbonate of soda.
½ level teaspoon ground cinnamon.
1 level dessertspoon ground ginger.
4 ozs. margarine.
8 ozs. soft brown sugar (pieces).
1 teacup dark treacle.
About 2 tablespoons evaporated milk.

Method: Grease several baking-tins and

set the oven at No. 3 or 4 (275°–300°F.). Sift the flour, salt, bicarbonate of soda, cinnamon and ginger into a bowl. Melt the margarine with the syrup and sugar—do not allow to boil. Cool a little and then pour onto the flour and other dry ingredients. Add enough milk to make into a firm pastry. Roll out and cut into shapes. Bake for 10 to 20 minutes until set.

SHREWSBURY BISCUITS

Ingredients:

    4 ozs. plain flour.
    2 ozs. margarine.
    1 yolk of egg (small).
    2 ozs. castor sugar.

Method: Cream the margarine and sugar until very light. Add a little of the egg yolk and some sifted flour alternately until all the flour is used up and a firm paste has been made—if the egg is large, all the yolk may not be needed. Set the paste aside in a cool place for about an hour. Roll out on a floured board and cut into shapes with a sharp cutter. Put on a greased tin and bake at No. 5 (375°F.) until pale-brown. If necessary, remove those on the outside of the tin before those in the centre. Turn the biscuits round to colour them evenly, but do not turn over. Above all, avoid over baking. The first biscuits should be ready in about ten minutes.

Cool on a wire tray until crisp. Store in an airtight tin, and decorate when needed.

Useful tracings can be taken from the following simple drawings, and used as a guide when making run-outs.

Be sure always to make a left and a right wing for a swan. The side next to the paper is placed against the swan's body, which must be run-out on both sides, the second side being completed only when the first is quite dry.

Two separate wings must be made for a butterfly (diag. 85). The body is not run-out, and is shown here only as a guide. It should be made of stiff icing straight onto the cake, the dry lace wings inserted carefully and propped with tissue-paper until dry. Vary the lace work, occasionally strengthening with solid run-out.

To stand upright, the ballet dancer (diag. 86) must be run-out on both sides, but only on one side if the figure is to be laid flat.

After running-out the numbers of flowers required, the petals of a wild rose (diag. 87) must be individually outlined to gain real effect. Also outline daisy and narcissus (diags. 88 & 89).

This is not necessary when making a pansy (diag. 90). Instead, the petals may be shaded, and the lines of the pansy "face" painted and accentuated with a little centre piping.

Further pictures can be traced from picture books, magazines and newspapers.

Use these letterings for run-out work, and if necessary embellish with dots and scrolls, or even tiny piped flowers. Other letters can be traced from cards, newspapers, books, etc.

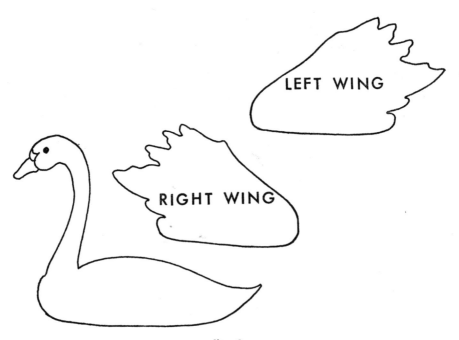

diag. 82

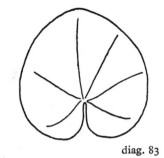

diag. 83

diag. 84

SOLID RUN OUT

diag. 85

diag. 86

diag. 87

diag. 88

diag. 89

diag. 90

diag. 91

Index

Page numbers are followed by 'a' to indicate the left-hand column and 'b' to indicate the right-hand column